INVENTORIES AND THE BUSINESS CYCLE

WITH SPECIAL REFERENCE TO CANADA

CANADIAN STUDIES IN ECONOMICS

A series of studies edited by V. W. Bladen, sponsored by the Canadian Social Science Research Council, and published with financial assistance from the Canada Council.

INVENTORIES
AND THE BUSINESS CYCLE
WITH SPECIAL REFERENCE
TO CANADA

By

CLARENCE L. BARBER

University of Manitoba

UNIVERSITY OF TORONTO PRESS: 1958

To My Father and Mother

PREFACE

This study falls into two parts. Part I contains a theoretical analysis of the relation of inventories and inventory fluctuations to the business cycle. It begins with a brief survey of the treatment of inventories in the literature on business cycles. Then a theoretical model of the economic system is developed as a basis for judging the nature and importance of inventory fluctuations in our economy. The initial model is that of an extremely simplified economy but, as the argument proceeds, these initial assumptions are gradually relaxed in order to provide an approximation to economic reality. In developing the model, use was made of relevant information about the behaviour of inventories and about the structure of an enterprise economy.

Part II is a study of inventory fluctuations in Canada over the period from 1918 to 1950 and provides some inductive verification of the preceding theoretical argument. The first chapter analyses in some detail the behaviour of inventories in ten important manufacturing industries. The second chapter contains an analysis of the movement of total inventories and of the behaviour of inventories in the main industrial subdivisions of the economy. A brief concluding chapter relates these findings to the theoretical analysis of Part I.

The earlier draft of this study, which was accepted by the University of Minnesota in partial fulfilment of the requirements for the degree of Doctor of Philosophy, has been modified to take account of some of the more recent work in this field and in a few instances some of the statistical information has been extended to cover more recent years. However, no attempt has been made to analyse the quarterly and monthly data on inventories which are now available for a fairly extended post-war period. Such an analysis must await a separate study.

In the preparation of this study I am particularly indebted to Mr. F. H. Leacy and Mr. J. B. Bergevin of the Dominion Bureau of Statistics for supplying me with their latest estimates and for answering all my queries promptly. I am also indebted to my thesis adviser Professor A. R. Upgren for his encouragement and advice.

CLARENCE BARBER

University of Manitoba

CONTENTS

TABLES

TABLES IN STATISTICAL APPENDIX

ILLUSTRATIONS

PART I

INVENTORY FLUCTUATIONS: A THEORETICAL ANALYSIS

CHAPTER ONE

THE ECONOMIC ROLE OF INVENTORIES

IN OUR ECONOMY inventories serve to bridge the gap between the production and sale of goods in much the same way that cash balances bridge the gap between the receipt and expenditure of income. Considerable time must elapse between the time that the output of a particular commodity is started and the time the commodity reaches the final consumer. In the meantime goods at various stages of completion exist in the form of inventories. These inventories fill what are often called the pipe-lines of our society.

The individual firm carries inventories for reasons of both necessity and convenience. A manufacturer must always carry a certain amount of goods in the actual process of manufacture. In addition, some raw materials will be "in process" in the sense that they are being unpacked, sorted, cleaned, and catalogued. Further, a certain volume of goods and materials is always in transit between various stages of production or distribution. A manufacturer will also want to carry sufficient stocks of materials to ensure the maintenance of a steady rate of production in the face of possible delays in the delivery of materials. Then, too, adequate inventories of materials allow a firm the convenience and lower expense of buying at less frequent intervals. Since minor variations in demand cannot be predicted exactly, a manufacturer will wish to carry a sufficient stock of finished goods to allow him to fill most orders promptly and thereby maintain the goodwill of his customers. A manufacturer who produces a variety of sizes or models of the same commodity needs a stock of finished goods to avoid too frequent changeovers in his production line; changeovers are costly because of the time lost in resetting machines. Retailers will also attempt to carry sufficient stocks to meet their customers' needs and offer them the opportunity of choosing from a wide variety of styles and patterns. Improvements in the speed of transportation and communication make it possible for manufacturers and merchants to carry smaller stocks and also reduce the volume of stocks in transit.

In all instances the advantages derived from carrying a larger inventory must be matched against the costs of doing so. A larger inventory involves added costs in the form of interest on the funds invested, insurance and storage charges, a risk of obsolescence or physical depreciation and of loss through a decline in prices. In some circumstances additional capital may not be available and any further investment in inventories will have to compete with other potential uses for the funds a firm has at its disposal. The importance of these costs varies for different categories of inventories. Although storage costs are small on most highly manufactured goods these are more subject to obsolescence and may not be easy to protect against a decline in price. In contrast, basic raw materials may involve higher storage costs unless the firm already has storage space available, but they are less subject to obsolescence and the firm may be able to protect itself against a decline in prices by hedging its purchases in commodity markets. Again, where goods are manufactured under binding orders, the risk of loss from a change in price is limited, for the firm can buy materials against each order.

The amount carried in stock by any firm will usually be capable of wide variation. One investigation has shown that stock-sales ratios in manufacturing typically decline when production is expanding and increase in periods when production is contracting.[1] Similar evidence will be presented at a later point in this study. This inverse movement could reflect a change in which business firms acquiesce because it cannot be easily avoided or it could result from a deliberate policy. Economists have not been in agreement on this point. Mr. Kalecki has suggested that retailers may attempt to attract more trade in periods of depression by stocking a wider variety of goods.[2] Mr. J. M. Clark, on the other hand, has argued that when times are bad merchants may be forced to economize by cutting down on the range of goods and styles they carry.[3] The availability of credit or investment funds would undoubtedly be a factor in their decision.

Since major firms have adopted better methods of controlling inventories during recent decades, it seems likely that the inverse movement of the stock-sales ratio may be the result, in part at least, of deliberate policy.[4] Thus, if quantity discounts, price anticipations, and safety allowances are excluded, it can be shown that the most economical quantity to purchase at one time varies directly with the square root of expected sales and the square root of procurement expense and varies inversely with the square root of carrying charges.[5] A similar relationship holds true for the most economical lot to manufacture before changing machines over to a different size or model of the product. The only difference in this latter instance is that the cost of changeover replaces procurement expense in the above formula. Since the size of inventory will vary directly with the quantity purchased or manufactured at one time, it is clear that if a firm were to follow the above formula, inventories would not increase in direct proportion to sales but only in proportion to the square root of sales. A fourfold increase in sales would only result in a twofold increase in inventories. The result is an inverse movement in the stock-sales ratio relative to sales or production. Moreover, Whitin has argued that even when allowance has been made for the factors excluded above—quantity discounts, price anticipations, and safety allowances—this result is not invalidated. Only if there were substantial stocking and destocking in anticipation of rising and falling prices would there be reason to expect a departure from the inverse movement of the stock-sales ratio. It is also true, as Abramovitz has pointed out, that because inventories typically lag behind production and sales at cyclical turning points, an inverse movement in the stock-sales ratio is bound to occur over at least part of the cycle.[6]

The ease with which individual firms can change their inventories or their stock-sales ratio depends on a number of circumstances. In the case of raw materials, the ability to increase stocks depends on how long is required between an increase in orders or purchases and actual delivery; the ability to decrease stocks on how quickly deliveries can be reduced after new orders are cut. The more distant the supplier and the slower the method of transport the longer these lags will be. In the case of finished goods, a reduction in stocks can be achieved by reducing output below the level of current sales; an increase in stocks by increasing output above the level of current sales. Technically, it is probably easier to reduce output than it is to increase it, for the latter may require the organization of increased production lines and the hiring and training of additional workers. Where manufacturers are producing to fill current orders, mistakes in predicting future sales may temporarily make it difficult to adjust inventories of finished goods to the desired level. In periods of intense activity when many goods are scarce there is a tendency for such inventories to decline to or below minimum working levels. During such periods, finished goods at any stage tend to move on quickly to the next stage and from the retailer into the hands of the consumer. In the early post-war period, when this was true, manufacturers often bought whatever materials were available because deliveries were uncertain. Frequent complaints of unbalanced inventories appeared in business journals. But in more normal periods, most individual firms can probably adjust their inventory after a short lag if they wish to do so. The extent to which all firms simultaneously can do the same will require further examination.

Seasonal variations in both production and demand call forth similar seasonal variations in inventories. The annual output of a commodity that is produced at one season of the year will be stored to meet a steady year-round consumption. This is true of most agricultural products. Similarly, where consumers' demand is seasonal, manufacturers will usually meet it by accumulating inventories in advance. The advance production of goods that are subject to rapid changes in style may be small, and manufacturers may rely on their ability to produce quickly to order in meeting current demand. But it may often be profitable for the manufacturer to meet a seasonal demand for more standardized goods by producing steadily throughout the year and accumulating stocks in periods of slack sales.

Finally, business firms may use their inventories as a method of earning speculative profits by anticipating changes in price. When prices are expected to rise, business firms will have an incentive to build up their inventories in order to liquidate them at a profit. When prices are expected to fall, business firms will attempt to keep their inventories at minimum working levels to avoid a loss on high cost inventory. How important this policy may be in causing an accumulation or liquidation of inventories cannot be easily determined. It has often been discussed in the literature on business cycles and it will be examined further in the next chapter.

CHAPTER TWO

THE TREATMENT OF INVENTORIES
IN BUSINESS CYCLE THEORY

NUMEROUS WRITERS on business cycle theory have discussed or commented on inventories though rarely systematically or at length. Despite the scattered nature of these comments there is evidence that some measure of agreement is beginning to develop on the nature and importance of inventory fluctuations. Nevertheless, there are still many unsettled issues.

There appears to be general agreement that inventories are an important factor in causing or accentuating the minor or forty-month cycle. Professor A. H. Hansen, for example, states that "not infrequently the minor setbacks experienced in the major upswings may be characterized as inventory recessions."[1] Similarly, Professor M. Abramovitz, after a detailed study of the behaviour of manufacturing inventories in the United States, concludes that "the prominence of inventory investment as an aggravating agent in short cycles may be considered as established."[2] Though leading theorists seem agreed that inventories are an important causal or aggravating agent in short cycles there is no agreement on their precise role. One group of economists believes that these minor cycles are involuntary oscillations. As a result of an initial increase in investment in durable assets, business firms find themselves faced with an involuntary decline in inventories. In their attempt to make good this deficiency and build their stocks up to a size needed at a higher sales level, they carry production to a level which they cannot sustain. As soon as they cease these planned additions to stocks they find themselves faced with a further involuntary increase in their inventory; the attempt to liquidate this leads to a recession.[3] According to a somewhat simpler view, the minor cycle is caused by the miscalculations of manufacturers who, in producing for sales expected several months later, periodically increase their output too rapidly. An accumulation of stocks results and a minor recession occurs while these stocks are being depleted.[4]

Still another explanation can be given in terms of the acceleration principle. During an expansion, increased investment in inventories will be required to provide the stocks needed for higher sales. But this investment is inevitably of a temporary nature. When the rate of growth of sales slows down or levels off, investment in inventories will begin to decline and may cease entirely. If this cessation of investment leads to a drop in income and expenditures, business firms may reduce their stocks, thus contributing to a minor recession.[5] Finally, it is possible for a minor recession to occur merely because business firms become apprehensive about the level of their stocks or about the future course of prices and attempt to liquidate some of their inventory by reducing their current rate of output or by cutting down on new orders. If the resulting fall in production and income causes a substantial recession, the fears of business would seem to have been justified. There is as yet no agreement on which of these theories best explains the role of inventories in minor cycles, though Abramovitz has advanced some evidence against Metzler's theory[6] Moreover, as

Hansen has argued, the role played by inventories may differ from one short cycle to another.

There is also general agreement among economists that the accumulation of inventories during a period of expansion and their liquidation during a period of contraction play an important part in accentuating major cyclical fluctuations. Thus Hansen has argued that, although inventories in the United States were not overextended in 1929, once the decline in activity had set in, disinvestment in inventories was induced by the decline in sales and this reinforced the downward movement in income and employment.[7] There is also considerable agreement that the cessation of disinvestment in inventories followed by an increase in output to the level of current sales may be an important factor in initiating a revival. In recent discussions it has been emphasized that this favourable effect will set in as soon as the rate of disinvestment begins to fall; it need not wait until disinvestment ceases entirely.[8]

Numerous writers have argued that, in periods of rising prices, speculative accumulations of stocks are likely to occur which will temporarily reinforce the price rise and may make a subsequent recession inevitable. Once prices begin to rise, it is argued, business firms will have an incentive to anticipate their purchases and speculators will buy commodities and hold them off the market. This is true to the extent that an initial rise in price is taken as an indication that prices are likely to rise further. Similarly, when prices are falling, business firms will expect a further price decline and will attempt to reduce their stocks to a minimum. Speculators will reinforce this movement by unloading their stocks.

Though this theory has had widespread support it is, in many respects, unsatisfactory. It implies that speculators and business men are invariably unsuccessful in their speculative operations. For, if commodities were purchased when prices were low and sold when prices were higher, this action would moderate the degree of price rise. With effective competition the amount earned would only cover the cost of carrying stocks from one period to another. It neglects the fact that business firms realize that prices may go down as well as up and may be very sensitive to the risk of being caught with large stocks in a period of falling prices. If the risk of loss is judged to be more serious than the opportunity for gain the result might be the reverse of that envisioned by these writers. Business firms may attempt to keep their stocks to a minimum when faced with rising prices. In industries where the risk of loss on stocks because of changes in price is severe, producers may protect themselves by hedging in the organized commodity markets. Moreover, speculators can operate most conveniently and with a minimum amount of funds in these same markets.

However, there is evidence that speculative accumulation of stocks has been important in some cycles. The period 1919-20 and, to a lesser extent, that of 1936-37 have been frequently cited as instances of inventory booms in the United States. Professor A. G. Hart has suggested that in the former case "people were willing to buy goods and hold goods at prices they thought were excessive because they counted on finding other people who were enough more foolish to take over the over-priced goods at still higher prices."[9] In the latter instance, the rapid accumulation of stocks has been blamed on the fear of interruptions of supply as a result of widespread strikes and the anticipation of increased labour costs.[10] Thus speculative accumulation of stocks may occasionally be an important factor in cyclical fluctuations but it seems probable that the importance of this factor has been over-emphasized. This appears to be the view of Abramovitz who argues that manufacturers may occasionally anticipate some purchases where price rises are expected, but they will avoid speculation on any extensive scale.[11]

Another argument, closely related to the above, concerns the effect of changing levels of prices on the inventory valuation and profits of business firms. Under the most widely used methods of inventory accounting, it is customary to calculate profits by charging the earliest purchases still on hand, rather than the materials that have been purchased most recently, to cost of goods sold. The effect of this practice, which will be discussed in more detail later, is to inflate profits in periods of rising prices and deflate them when prices are falling. This bit of self-deception results in business firms feeling more optimistic in periods of rising prices, paying out more money as dividends and spending more for capital expansion. The reverse is true in periods of falling prices. If profits were calculated as they should be, according to these writers, by charging current purchases against sales, a good deal of stability would be added to our economic system. This argument is parallel to the one discussed above, for it can be argued that the profits which tempt business firms to anticipate their purchases in a period of rising prices are mainly paper profits, at least for any firm that is in business on a continuing basis.[12]

A special theory about the role of inventories in the trade cycle was developed by the late Lord Keynes. In his *Treatise on Money* Keynes distinguished between working capital and liquid capital or surplus stocks.[13] Working capital was defined to include all inventories which were essential to the production and distribution of goods. Any inventories in excess of this amount he called liquid capital. According to Keynes, in the initial stages of any slump there will be some accumulation of liquid capital which will offset the reduction in working capital and this will moderate the decline in activity. But because of the heavy costs of carrying surplus stocks an intense effort will be made to liquidate them. Prices will fall until either consumption increases or production falls off sufficiently to absorb these surplus stocks. Once they are absorbed, recovery is likely to set in, but because all liquid capital has been eliminated, the rate of recovery will be retarded by the necessity of building up working capital. If liquid capital were available it could be readily converted into working capital, but, according to Keynes, most of the liquid capital will have been wiped out in the slump. Thus the effort to get rid of surplus stocks intensifies the cyclical downswing and the success of this effort operates to retard the upswing.

Keynes appears to have retained this theory without substantial modification in his later book.[14] There he argued that the time required to absorb surplus stocks, a period he estimated at from three to five years, was an important factor in determining the length of the cycle. As R. G. Hawtrey has pointed out, this theory applies most readily to primary commodities; it probably reflects Keynes' work in that field.[15] It does not apply equally to manufactured products where carrying costs are frequently much lower and prices are generally much more stable.[16] Moreover, even in the field of primary commodities, as will be shown below, Keynes' theory does not fit the facts particularly well.

Mr. Hawtrey is another theorist who has given considerable attention to the role of inventories in the business cycle.[17] Although usually regarded as a writer who holds a purely monetary cycle theory, his explanation of the way an expansion and contraction of bank credit occurs centres around the efforts of wholesalers to add to or reduce their stocks. Wholesale merchants, he argues, operate on a narrow margin of profit and for this reason their demand for stocks is sensitive to a change in the short-term rate of interest. Thus, if the banks reduce the rate of interest, these traders will be induced to increase their orders for goods. At this point Hawtrey makes an assumption which most present-day economists find difficult to accept: that all the income earned in producing goods to meet these new orders is spent either for consumer goods or for long-term capital expansion. None of it, he appears to argue, will be available to finance increased inventories. Accordingly, inventories can only accumulate to the extent that part of the additional income is retained in the form of the larger cash balances needed at a higher income level, or, as he expresses it, to the extent that the economy absorbs cash. Because of increased expenditures wholesalers find their stocks declining instead of increasing as they had planned. Accordingly they increase their orders even further thus causing a cumulative expansion. The initial decline in wholesale stocks will be counterbalanced by increased stocks at earlier stages of production and there will be some over-all increase in stocks as the economy absorbs cash.

Hawtrey believes, in contrast to Keynes, that output can be increased at all stages of production more or less simultaneously so that the wholesaler will soon be receiving increased supplies. If stocks at retail or wholesale levels begin to get unduly low, they will defend them by raising their prices, but he does not think price rises will be extensive until output approaches capacity in most industries. At this stage, anticipated rises in price will provide the wholesaler with a further incentive for attempting to increase his stocks. Though Hawtrey's theory envisons some increase in stocks during the course of an expansion, he argues that total stocks will still be below normal in relation to sales when a restriction of credit causes the expansion to give way to contraction.[18] Thus actual investment and disinvestment in stocks play a relatively small role in Mr. Hawtrey's theory. It is the attempted expansion and attempted liquidation of stocks in the face of continual disappointment that is the moving force.

Mr. Hawtrey's theory has been most widely criticized on the grounds that he over-emphasizes the extent to which wholesale inventories are sensitive to the rate of interest. Though the weight of opinion appears to be against Mr. Hawtrey on this point, the evidence is not conclusive.[19] His most valuable contribution to the theory of inventory fluctuations is his emphasis on the extent to which planned investment in inventories may not be realized in the process of an expansion or contraction of income. In this respect his theory is similar to Professor Metzler's work on inventory cycles.[20]

In two further theories of the cycle, the level of inventories appears more as a symptom than as a cause. According to one, the over-production theory, the climax of a boom is characterized by an over-production of goods of all types. According to the other, the monetary over-investment theory, almost the exact opposite prevails; at the peak of the boom there is a shortage of all types of consumer goods and their prices are rising.

Numerous writers have advanced an over-production theory of the cycle and Hawtrey states that a form of this theory was "the explanation of the trade cycle prevalent among what I may call the classical school of economists.[21] Different writers have emphasized different factors as the prime cause of over-production. According to Mr. W. H. Beveridge, it arises because numerous small firms unaware of each other's plans tend to overshoot the market and preduce a glut of goods. After this glut is worked off a period of shortage follows until another burst of competition produces another glut.[22] Professor C. O. Hardy presents a similar theory in which he emphasizes the fact that the risk of over-production has been increased by the uncertainty connected with the long period of time involved in the capitalistic method of production. Over-production is also encouraged by the purchases of speculators seeking a gain from rising prices.[23] Professor A. C. Pigou also supports a form of this theory and quotes from Hardy with approval.[24] In Pigou's view periods of over-production followed by under-production are accentuated by alternate waves of optimism and pessimism among business firms. Cycle theories involving over-production and the accumulation of stocks of goods have also been presented by Frank, Mitchell, Hobson, and Aftalion.[25]

The leading exponent of the monetary over-investment theory is Professor F. A. Hayek.[26] According to his theory, entrepreneurs are first lured into starting more roundabout capitalistic methods of production because they can borrow from the banking system at a low rate of interest. Eventually additional bank credit is unavailable and a relative rise in consumer expenditures begins to attract resources away from the capital goods industry forcing an abandonment of the new methods of production. By implication, stocks of consumer goods must be very low at this stage; otherwise there would be no need to attract resources away from other industry. Both the preceding theories have been subjected to severe criticism and receive little support at the present time; at best they offer a very partial explanation of what happens in the course of a business cycle.

In his recent monumental study of manufacturing inventories in the United States, Abramovitz has shown that investment in manufacturing inventories typically reaches its peaks and troughs at the same time as manufacturing output and business activity in general.[27] Yet if investment in inventories were to behave in the manner suggested by the acceleration principle it should reach its peaks and troughs at the same time as the *rate of change* in rather than the *volume* of manufacturing output. By means of a careful analysis Abramovitz was able to show that the rate of increase in manufacturing output usually reaches a maximum well before the end of an expansion and that its rate of decline reaches a maximum sometime before the end of a contraction. Thus, investment in inventories lags well behind the rate of change in output. There is a similar discrepancy between the expected and actual behaviour of the total volume of manufacturing inventories. For while the pure theory of the accelerator would lead one to expect that the peaks and troughs in manufacturing inventories would coincide with the peaks and troughs of total output, Abramovitz finds that manufacturing inventories lag from six to twelve months at cyclical turning points. This lag is consistent with the cyclical behaviour of investment in inventories.

To explain these findings Abramovitz resorts to a detailed analysis of different types of manufacturing inventories. Though in the course of his analysis he distinguishes between eight different categories of inventory, in his final summing up he rests his conclusions primarily on the behaviour of four major groups: goods in process; finished goods made to order; raw materials; and finished goods sold from stock. The first two of these groups, which are estimated to comprise 25 to 30 per cent of all manufacturing inventories, tend to move almost simultaneously with output, goods in process showing a short lead and finished goods made to order a short lag. Inventories of these two groups behave in the way the theory of the accelerator would lead one to expect, with total inventories reaching their peaks and troughs at the same time as output, and investment in inventories showing a long lead at cyclical turning points.

Abramovitz shows that in respect to about three-fourths of the total inventories for raw materials, which constitute some 40 per cent of manufacturing inventories, manufacturers are able to adjust their stocks to changes in output with a short lag, perhaps three or four months. As for the other one-fourth, the long distance from which materials come, long-term contracts or other special conditions make it impossible for manufacturers to adjust their inventories promptly to changes in output, and inventories in this category show a substantial lag, in some instances from one to two years or more at cyclical turning points. On the basis of this analysis he concludes that total stocks of raw materials lag the turning points in the cycle by several months and that investment in raw materials leads. Though this lead is smaller than that shown by the rate of change in output it is still a significant though uncertain amount (perhaps six months).

In contrast to the behaviour of raw materials, most finished goods sold from stock move in a counter-cyclical fashion, although when the expansion or contraction is long (two years or more), they may reverse direction and move in the same direction as manufacturing activity. Investment in this category of inventory increases rapidly as a contraction commences and then levels off. The rate of investment may decline before an upturn occurs and Abramovitz advances some reasons for expecting such a result, but except in long contractions, the evidence is not clear. During an expansion the rate of investment first declines rapidly and then levels off. In long expansions the rate of liquidation declines and some accumulation occurs; but in moderately long or short expansions it is not certain that the rate of investment rises prior to the cyclical downturn.

The behaviour of manufacturer's inventories as a whole, Abramovitz suggests, can be explained in terms of the combined effects of these diverse movements in different categories of inventory. In the opening stages of a contraction, investment in the first two groups—goods in process and finished goods made to order—falls rapidly, investment in raw materials also declines though less rapidly, but these declines are offset by a rapid accumulation of finished goods made for stock. Towards the middle of the contraction the rate of investment in inventories is still declining as the rate of investment in the first three groups continues to fall while the rate of accumulation of finished goods made to stock begins to level off. Again, towards the end of the contraction the rate of investment in the first two groups may begin to rise a little but investment in raw materials probably continues to fall and investment in finished goods made to order may also begin to decline as manufacturers resist further accumulations. Thus investment in inventories as a whole continues to fall until the end of the contraction. The reverse pattern occurs during an expansion.

One weakness in this explanation is its failure to distinguish between intentional and involuntary changes in inventory. It is clear that the changes in inventory of goods in process and in stocks of finished goods made to order are largely intentional. Again, Abramovitz suggests that for some three-fourths of the total, changes in raw materials inventory are largely intentional except for a short lag. For the remaining one-fourth the changes that occur may either be intentional with a long lag, or, as is true with crude rubber stocks, completely involuntary. But it is not at all clear whether the accumulation in the important groups of durable finished goods sold from stock that occurs during a contraction is intentional, in the sense that manufacturers could avoid it if they were to reduce their output more promptly or cut their prices to clear surplus stocks, or whether it reflects an accumulation which manufacturers are unable to avoid. Professor R. Nurkse has taken Abramovitz to task for his failure to explore this question further and in particular for his failure to investigate the extent to which any planned changes in inventories may be self-defeating because of the effects they will have on income and expenditure.[28]

Abramovitz contends that the continued growth in inventory investment even after the rate of growth in output has begun to decline moderates and lengthens business expansions. Similarly, the lag in inventory investment behind the rate of change in output moderates and lengthens a contraction. Nurkse has questioned this conclusion and constructed a particular model sequence in which this effect is not present. Nurkse's argument is not conclusive, however, for he admits the particular assumptions upon which his model is based are not realistic. Abramovitz's argument here seems to imply that the continued accumulations or reductions in inventory that lengthen the cyclical expansion and contraction are intentional. To the extent that the lag in adjusting raw material stocks is involved, this is probably true. But if the inventory changes are to any substantial extent unintentional, as the changes in supplies of finished goods may be, only in a very limited sense can it be argued that they moderate and lengthen the cyclical phase.

Though annual data indicate that investment in inventories shows neither a lead nor a lag at cyclical turning points, Abramovitz admits that if adequate monthly data were available a lead might be revealed indicating that changes in the rate of investment in inventories were a causal factor at cyclical turning points. Further, as Nurkse has noted, planned or intended investment in inventories may decline before the peak or trough of a cycle even though actual realized investment reaches its peak and trough at the same time as total output.

Abramovitz also demonstrates that changes in investment in inventories are more important in short than in long contractions or expansions and shows clearly why this result could be expected. Since the rate of investment in inventories at the trough and peak of the cycle is independent of its length it is clear that the total increase or decrease in this investment will be smaller in relation to the change in gross national product the longer the expansion or contraction involved (on the assumption, which is usually valid, that the amount of change in gross national product is correlated with the length of the cyclical phase). His data also show that over the period from 1919 to 1938 changes in investment in inventories have been much more important during periods of contraction than during periods of expansion, accounting on the average for 47.5 per cent of the change in gross national product during periods of contraction and only 23.3 per cent during periods of expansion. Though various explanations of this difference have been advanced, it seems probable that it is mainly a reflection of the upward trend in gross national product. Over the five cycles from 1919 to 1938 in the United States, the growth in gross national product (in 1929 dollars) averaged $12.1 billion compared with an average decline during contractions of $7.2 billion. Since there is no reason to expect a comparable asymmetry between the change in inventories during expansions and contractions the natural result is that the smaller base against which the change in investment in inventories is measured during contractions gives a larger percentage.

On the basis of an analysis of Abramovitz's data, Nurkse has suggested that the passive decumulations during a revival are larger and more prolonged than the periods of passive accumulation in the early stages of a downswing. He suggests that this may be accounted for in part by the fact that it is less difficult technically for business men to reduce their output promptly at the onset of a contraction than it is to increase it when revival gets underway, and in part by the fact that business men view with more alarm an unwanted accumulation of stocks than they do an undesired reduction and will make more strenuous efforts to avoid it.

CHAPTER THREE

INVENTORY FLUCTUATIONS IN A SIMPLE MODEL
OF THE ECONOMIC SYSTEM

IN ORDER TO ANALYSE the part played by inventories in the business cycle it is convenient to develop a simplified model of the economic system which, as the analysis proceeds, is made more complex in an attempt to approach economic reality as closely as possible. The model is developed in terms of an enterprise system similar to that now prevailing in Canada and the United States. Changes in the level of income and employment in such an economy are primarily the result of the decisions of individuals, business firms, and governments. Individuals affect the flow of income and expenditure by their decisions to accept employment on certain terms and to spend at a certain rate and at a certain time; business firms by their decisions to produce or not produce, to buy capital goods or raw materials, to offer certain wage rates, and to set certain prices on their finished products. Some changes in government expenditures and revenues occur automatically as a result of established expenditure programmes or taxes; others occur rather infrequently or on more or less fixed occasions as is true of the annual budget.

The distinction between the decisions of individuals and the decisions of business firms deserves emphasis. For a large part of the economy's output the decision to increase or decrease production is made by the business firm. If individual business men decide to increase production by hiring additional employees and purchasing more material, the result is a rise in the gross national product. The second type of decision, the decision of individuals to buy consumer goods or services or of the business firm to buy capital equipment, will be affected by the increased income that accompanies this rise in production. These latter expenditures in turn affect the profitability of the business firm's operations and modify its decisions accordingly. The interaction of the two chief types of decisions has a marked effect on the cyclical behaviour of inventories.

A form of period analysis involving definite clock-time periods of one month has been adopted. In thus selecting among the many types of period analysis available the governing considerations were first, the desire to make the model correspond as closely with the real world as possible, and second, the need to avoid concealing any of the dynamic development which occurs.[1] A clock-time period of one month satisfies both of these criteria to a considerable extent.[2] Actual economic events all occur during definite clock-time periods and the statistical record of these events is also of this type. For a period of one month there is now much statistical data available. For shorter periods than this, a week or a day, the amount of statistical data is much scantier, and, because of irregular and seasonal movements in many types of data, it may often be difficult to distinguish irregular or seasonal fluctuation in a given series from an underlying cyclical development; even for a period as long as a month this difficulty arises. On the other hand, for a period longer than a month there is more danger of concealing part of the dynamic development within the cycle. For a period as long as a year, which completely avoids the seasonal problem, it frequently happens that one period records the result of diverse movements in the data during the year. This is especially true when the year coincides with a turning point in the business cycle. A three month period is less likely to average out important changes and the availability of estimates of gross national product on this basis argue in its favour. However, where the need arises, monthly periods can be combined into quarters.

Another important consideration in selecting a period for any dynamic sequence is the timing and frequency of the decisions which change the course of economic events. The most important of these are the decisions business men make in regard to their volume of employment and production, the decisions of consumers regarding the allocation of their income and the interaction between these two sets of decisions.[3] A period of one month seemed to strike a happy medium; it is long enough to allow for changes in the decisions of a majority of business men and yet short enough to reveal any important interaction between consumers' spending decisions and business men's production and employment decisions. Most business firms make use of a monthly sales and income statement for their own purposes. Though some of the larger firms obtain data weekly on at least part of their production and sales, the irregularities which may occur on a week-to-week basis make it unlikely that, business decisions will be changed that frequently. However, use of a period of one month for an important part of the analysis does not mean that longer periods may not be important for some types of decisions. Thus the decision to build a new factory or buy new machinery may respond less quickly to changes in economic events than other types of decisions. Similarly the decision to use a clock-time period does not prevent the use of other types of periods for analytical purposes. It simply requires that such periods, for example the gestation periods, must be linked up to clock-time.

In the analysis that follows, use is made of a model of the Keynesian type. Savings for any period are defined as income less consumption. Accordingly, investment including changes in inventories must always be equal to savings. Initially, all investment expenditures except investment in inventories are assumed to be autonomous or non-induced, that is, independent of the level of income. This assumption will be modified later. Saving and consumption, on the other hand, are each assumed to be a fairly stable function of income; saving and consumption in this sense refer to the amounts the community would attempt to save and consume at each income level provided that the given income level were to persist. Accordingly, they can be represented as schedules relating consumption and saving to income, just as a demand schedule relates quantity demanded to price. In this situation a condition of equilibrium is that in which the amount people wish to save exactly equals the amount business firms and individuals are willing to invest. If this is not true at the existing income level, income will change until the two are brought into equality. Equilibrium will exist at that income where the savings and investment schedules intersect and this equilibrium will be stable provided the investment schedule intersects the savings schedule from above (income being measured on the x axis). Given a stable savings schedule, the equilibrium level of income will be that income level towards which the economy tends to move as a result of any independent change in the level of investment expenditures.

While the amount business firms and individuals are willing to invest and the amount the community attempts to save will usually be equal at one or, at the most, a few income levels, the actual amount of saving and investment realized must always be equal. This apparent paradox can be explained by two factors. In any period, actual saving may differ from the amount people would like to save at that income level because of unexpected increases in income which are almost entirely saved even though they may lead to increased expenditure in subsequent periods. Similarly the amount business firms and individuals would like to invest at a given income level may differ from actual investment because of unexpected changes in inventories. Both of these factors, the unexpected changes in income and the unexpected changes in inventories, will lead to actions in subsequent periods which will help restore income to an equilibrium level. Thus unexpected increases in income, which remain unspent at the end of a period, are likely to lead to an increase in expenditure during succeeding periods. Similarly, unexpected decreases in the volume of inventories held at the end of a period are likely to lead to an attempt to replace them in a later period. These considerations are equally applicable to unexpected losses or to increases in stocks in the face of a decline in sales. The unexpected changes in inventories are of particular importance from the standpoint of this study. The level of inventories will only remain constant or correspond to the planned level if sales correspond to the expectations of business firms.[4]

For convenience, savings, consumption, and investment in the schedule sense will be referred to as planned savings, planned consumption, and planned investment respectively. In meaning they correspond exactly with what Hansen has called "desired saving," "desired consumption," and "intended investment."[5] They are to be distinguished from actual or realized saving and investment, which must always be equal, and from unplanned saving or dissaving due to unexpected changes in income and from unplanned investment or disinvestment due to unexpected changes in inventories. Some objections can be raised to the terms "planned" and "unplanned"; for example, planned saving may include some saving out of income which was not foreseen in advance and hence in this sense is unplanned. However, as long as it is kept clearly in mind that the term planned as used here refers to savings, consumption, and investment in the schedule sense there should be no confusion.

Within this framework a somewhat lengthy list of assumptions has been adopted for the first model. The results obtained at this level of abstraction will be modified considerably as the analysis approaches more closely to reality, and each assumption will be examined critically at the point in the analysis where it is modified. In the initial model the following assumptions are made: It is a closed economy; there are no government receipts or expenditures; interest rates remain constant; changes in income and expenditure affect employment and production without changing prices; all incomes are paid out in the period earned and spent in that period without any lag, all consumers' expenditures are made on goods sold out of inventories; inventories are valued at selling prices so that an increase in consumers spending results in an exactly equivalent decline in inventories; investment expenditures on plant and equipment are fully realized in the period in which they are made, that is, there is no change in the level of inventories as a direct result of these expenditures; except where definite assumptions are made, investment in plant and equipment is assumed to be constant and independent of other components of income; the average and the marginal propensity to consume are both constant and equal to 80 per cent of income received and remain the same during both an expansion and a contraction; total income (G.N.P.) is defined to include depreciation and similar capital consumption allowances and is equal to investment in plant and equipment (I), plus consumers' expenditures (C), plus net change in inventories (N); total inventories are designated by (H) and production of consumer goods, valued at sales prices, by (P); in each period (N) will equal (P) minus (C). Investment in plant and equipment includes all private investment except investment in inventories and is sometimes referred to as investment in durable assets. The first model will be referred to as Model 1.

Starting from an equilibrium position let us first consider the effects of an independent increase in investment expenditures to a level 100 higher than at the beginning (period 1). Manufacturers of consumer goods, it is assumed, attempt to produce an amount equal to the sales of the preceding period. Thus, in period 2 of Table 1, income has increased by 100 as a result of the increase in investment expenditures. This leads to an increase in consumers' expenditures of 80 in the same period. Since the production of consumer goods has not changed, inventories of consumer goods will decline by an equal amount. In period 3, producers of consumer goods increase their output sufficiently to meet the sales level of the preceding period. But this increased output and income of 80 leads to a further increase in consumers' spending within the period amounting to 64 (that is, 80 per cent of 80). Thus consumers' spending still exceeds the output of goods and a further decline in inventories occurs.

In this model it is apparent that by the time the final level of income was reached total inventories would have declined by 400, exactly the amount by which consumption per period has increased. The steps in this process correspond in amount to those in the usual statement of the multiplier.[6] However, it is highly unrealistic to assume that entrepreneurs would allow their inventories

TABLE 1

A Multiplier Sequence with Declining Inventories

Monthly periods	I	P	N	C	G.N.P.	H
1	1,000	4,000	0	4,000	5,000	3,000
2	1,100	4,000	—80	4,080	5,100	2,920
3	1,100	4,080	—64	4,144	5,180	2,856
4	1,100	4,144	—51	4,195	5,244	2,805
Final level	1,100	4,400	0	4,400	5,500	2,600

I — Investment in plant and equipment; P — Production of consumer goods; N — Net change in inventories; C — Consumer expenditures; G.N.P. — Total income = P + I = I + N + C; H — Total inventories.

to decline continuously in this fashion without making some effort to replace them. If we assume that entrepreneurs increase their production in each period sufficiently not only to meet the sales level of the preceding period but also to replace all the reduction in inventories that has occurred, we obtain the results shown in Table 2. In period 4, for example, output of consumer goods increases sufficiently to meet the sales level in the preceding period, 4208, and to replace the reduction in inventory that has occurred since the initial position, namely 80 plus 48. The sum of these three, 4208 plus 80 plus 48, equals 4336.

Examination of Table 2 indicates that an equilibrium level of income is not approached in a smooth manner, rather cyclical fluctuations of gradually decreasing amplitude develop. An initial decline in the level of inventories is followed by an accumulation which continues beyond the point where the original level of inventories is restored (period 8). At this stage, business firms attempt to reduce their production to keep their inventories at the original level but the concurrent decline in sales causes a continued accumulation of inventories which only stops when the level of income falls to the equilibrium level

TABLE 2

A Simple Inventory Cycle

Monthly periods	I	P	N	C	G.N.P.	H	Np*
1	1,000	4,000		4,000	5,000	3,000	0
2	1,100	4,000	—80	4,080	5,100	2,920	0
3	1,100	4,160	—48	4,208	5,260	2,872	80
4	1,100	4,336	—13	4,349	5,436	2,859	128
5	1,100	4,490	18	4,472	5,590	2,877	141
6	1,100	4,595	39	4,556	5,695	2,916	123
7	1,100	4,640	48	4,592	5,740	2,964	84
8	1,100	4,628	46	4,582	5,728	3,010	36
9	1,100	4,572	34	4,538	5,672	3,044	—10
10	1,100	4,494	19	4,475	5,594	3,063	—44
11	1,100	4,412	2	4,410	5,512	3,065	—63
12	1,100	4,345	—11	4,356	5,445	3,054	—65
13	1,100	4,302	—20	4,322	5,402	3,034	—54
14	1,100	4,288	—22	4,310	5,388	3,012	—34
15	1,100	4,298	—20	4,318	5,398	2,992	—12

* Np—Planned investment in inventories.

(5,500). But at this level of income (period 11) the volume of inventories is now too high, and the attempt to reduce them will carry income below the equilibrium level. The disinvestment in inventories reduces the level of net total investment and this reduction has a downward multiplier effect. Once the level of stocks has been reduced to the normal level and the planned production in stocks ceases, income begins to rise again (period 14), but as long as income remains below the equilibrium level a further involuntary reduction in stocks occurs.[7]

An analysis of the above table makes it clear that our original equilibrium condition, the equality of planned saving and planned investment, will only be a condition for stable equilibrium if planned investment includes either a constant rate of planned investment in inventories or no planned investment in inventories with total inventories at a satisfactory level so that no further investment in inventories will be attempted.[8] If this further condition of equilibrium is not fulfilled the attempt to increase or decrease inventories will raise or lower the level of income but this new level of income will remain only as long as the investment or disinvestment in inventories continues. It is this twofold requirement of equilibrium which causes the cyclical pattern in Table 2.

It is evident from this model that the amount of inventory accumulation which occurs during any period of time may differ substantially from that planned by producers. A planned increase or decrease in inventories causes a corresponding change in income and subsequent expenditures out of this income cause the realized change in inventories to differ from the planned change. Furthermore, in this model no accumulation of inventories whether planned or unplanned can occur until the level of income exceeds the equilibrium level of income determined by the level of investment in durable assets and no reduction in inventories can occur until the level of income falls below this equilibrium level of income. More generally, whenever the level of income is below the equilibrium level of income determined by planned investment in durable assets, a reduction in inventories will occur; whenever it is above this level inventories will accumulate. It can easily be proved that this must be true. Savings are equal to investment by definition and since there are no lags in expenditure, planned savings will always be equal to actual savings. But planned savings and planned investment in durable assets are equal only at the equilibrium level of income. At lower income levels, planned investment in durable assets will exceed planned and actual savings by the net reduction in inventories. At income levels above the equilibrium level, planned investment in durable assets will be less than planned and actual savings by the net accumulation of inventory.

Thus in Table 2 with investment in durable assets of 1,100 and an average and marginal propensity to consume of .8 the equilibrium level of income is 5,500. It will be observed that whenever the income level is above 5,500 inventories are accumulating, whenever it falls below this level inventories are declining.

In this model the rate of investment in inventories reaches its peak and trough in the same period as the level of income. In this respect the model is consistent with the conclusions reached by Abramovitz. However, planned investment in inventories reaches its peak and trough two periods ahead of the level of income. Thus the fact that realized investment in inventories shows neither a lead nor lag at cyclical turning points in this model is entirely due to the unintended component of inventories. This would suggest that Abramovitz's conclusions are entirely consistent with a lead at cyclical turning points for planned changes in inventory.[9] It should also be noted that the level of inventories lags about one-quarter cycle behind the changes in income, reaching its peaks and troughs four periods later. This corresponds to a lag of four months in our model. However, the assumption that business men adjust their production plans with a lag of one month is not a precise one. If the adjustment period is longer than this the lag in this model would be quite consistent with Abramovitz's finding that manufacturers' inventories lag from six to twelve months at cyclical turning points.

In multiplier analysis it is often assumed that income and expenditure increase by a slow step-by-step process. This need not be the case. If business men anticipate the effects of the increase in income resulting from the rise in investment expenditures and simultaneously increase their production, the only limit on the rate of expansion outside of the optimism of business firms would be the technical one, the rate at which it is possible to hire additional labour and obtain added material. If raw materials and labour were plentiful, and if business men increased their production rapidly, the final equilibrium level might be reached in the second period. Thus, in the previous example, if business men had increased their production to 4,400 in the second period, they would have anticipated correctly the final sales level and no decline in inventories would have occurred.[10] In general, whenever an increase in investment occurs, the more rapidly business men increase their production, the smaller will be the decline in inventories which occurs before the equilibrium level of income is reached, and the more rapidly the latter will be approached. It is difficult to see how the multiplier can tell anything about the rate at which the new equilibrium level of income will be reached. In its step-by-step form it defines little more than the minimum rate of expansion.[11] A careful examination of past experience might shed some light on how fast an expansion or contraction in income and employment is likely to proceed. One group of economists has suggested that "only an aggregate of demand large enough to put strong upward pressure on prices is likely to be adequate for rapid re-employment."[12] Under these conditions the expectations of the business firms are likely to be extremely favourable. In the reconversion period following World War II business firms were willing to increase their employment very rapidly because, with price control still in effect, they anticipated a strong demand. But favourable business expectations could occur in other conditions and might create their own strong aggregate demand. During an expansion, technical factors such as the availability of skilled labour, machine tools, or productive capacity may limit the rate at which production can increase. In a contraction period there are fewer technical limitations on the rate of decline, and for that reason a contraction may often proceed more rapidly than an expansion.

Professor Metzler has developed further a model similar to the one discussed above by introducing a coefficient of expectations.[13] His coefficient of expectations relates business firms' expectations regarding the sale of consumer goods to the change in sales in the two preceding periods. If the coefficient of expectations is one, business firms will expect sales to increase during the following period by the same amount as they increased between the preceding period and the current period. The coefficient of expectations is assumed to remain constant throughout. He has shown that the introduction of a coefficient of expectations in the model discussed in Table 2 causes a cycle which fluctuates more violently but with a shorter period. Where both the propensity to consume and the coefficient of expectations are large (close to one) the system becomes unstable and fluctuates in cycles of gradually increasing amplitude. An example of the stable form of this cycle is given in Table 3. It is assumed here that the marginal propensity to consume is .8 and the coefficient of expectations is .5. Manufacturers attempt to produce enough in each period to meet the expected sales level and to restore inventories to their original level. Thus in period 3 producers expect a sales level of 4,120, that is, one equal to the sales level of period 2 (4,080) plus one-half of the increase in the preceding period (40). In addition, they produce an additional 80 to replace the decline in inventory which occurred in period 2.

The cycle appearing in this table is in sharp contrast with the conclusions reached above. In Professor Metzler's model, expectations make the cycle more pronounced though of shorter duration than in his original model. I have argued that the introduction of expectations might cause the cycle to disappear completely. The reason for this difference is essentially as follows Professor Metzler does not allow any increase in the production of consumer goods to occur until after the increase in investment expenditures is under way and this in turn has caused consumers' expenditures to increase and inventories to suffer an initial

TABLE 3

The Inventory Cycle with a Coefficient of Expectations

Monthly periods	I	P	N	C	G.N.P.	H	Np
1	1,000	4,000	0	4,000	5,000	3,000	0
2	1,100	4,000	—80	4,080	5,100	2,920	0
3	1,100	4,200	—40	4,240	5,300	2,880	80
4	1,100	4,440	8	4,432	5,540	2,888	120
5	1,100	4,640	48	4,592	5,740	2,936	112
6	1,100	4,736	67	4,669	5,836	3,003	64
7	1,100	4,705	61	4,644	5,805	3,042	—3

decline. Subsequently production plans are based on the expectation that the increase in sales of the preceding period will be repeated and on the desire to restore inventories to their original level. These are, as the author recognizes, oversimplified assumptions but he believes the results correspond fairly well with reality. In the discussion of the model in this chapter it was assumed that the output of consumer goods increases simultaneously with the rise in investment expenditures. If both increase simultaneously and at about the same rate it is suggested that output could rise to a level of full employment without any unexpected changes in inventories and without any involuntary inventory cycle. Moreover, it has been argued that even when an initial unexpected decline in inventories occurs this can be very rapidly restored if producers increase their output quickly enough.

The model used above can be equally well adapted to analysing a decline in income and expenditure. An example of this is given in Table 4 where a contraction in investment to a level 100 below that of period 1 is assumed. Business firms are assumed to produce an amount equal to their sales in the preceding period.

TABLE 4

The Multiplier Effects of a Decline in Investment

Monthly periods	I	P	N	C	G.N.P.	H
1	1,000	4,000	0	4,000	5,000	3,000
2	900	4,000	80	3,920	4,900	3,080
3	900	3,920	64	3,856	4,820	3,144
Final level	900	3,600	0	3,600	4,500	3,400

The results are analogous to those obtained in Table 1. The new equilibrium level of income would be 4,500 and as the level of income declined there would be a continuous rise in inventories, a rise amounting to 400 by the time the new equilibrium level of income was reached. But here again it is unrealistic to assume that business firms would allow inventories to accumulate at this rate without making some attempt to cut production more sharply. If the assumption is made that business firms attempt to meet the sales level of the preceding period and try to reduce inventories to their initial level, an inventory cycle similar to that in Table 2 appears. Income will decline below and then gradually approach the new lower equilibrium level in a cyclical pattern, with the cycle centred around the new lower equilibrium level of income. Here again the new equilibrium level of income will only be a stable equilibrium if inventories are at a satisfactory level.

So far our discussion has centred on the effects of adjustments in the level of inventories where the change in income resulted from a prior change in investment in durable assets. Let us now consider the effects of the decision of business firms to build up their inventories. In Table 5 business firms plan to increase their inventories by 100 per period.

TABLE 5

Planned Investment in Inventories

Monthly periods	I	P	N	C	G.N.P.	H
1	1,000	4,000	0	4,000	5,000	3,000
2	1,000	4,100	20	4,080	5,100	3,020
3	1,000	4,200	40	4,160	5,200	3,060
4	1,000	4,300	60	4,240	5,300	3,120
5	1,000	4,400	80	4,320	5,400	3,200
6	1,000	4,500	100	4,400	5,500	3,300

In this sequence, business firms discover in the initial stages that their plans do not quite succeed because the unexpected increase in sales prevents them from increasing their inventories to the extent they had planned. Under these circumstances, if they are still intent on adding to their inventories at the original rate they can be expected to increase their production more rapidly. Thus the required level of inventory accumulation can be attained in the second period if they increase their production of consumer goods to 4,500 at once. At this level of income the monthly investment in inventories will just offset the increased saving out of this higher level of income. But inventory accumulation cannot continue indefinitely and when firms decide to discontinue it and reduce their production accordingly, they find their plans thwarted again. For every reduction of 100 in production of consumer goods there will be a corresponding decline of 80 in consumer expenditure so that the net reduction in the rate of inventory accumulation will be only 20. This is illustrated in Table 6, a continuation of Table 5.

This Table shows that the attempted cessation of inventory accumulation will start a decline in income and employment which will continue until the lower equilibrium level is reached again. During the decline, inventories will continue to accumulate and if, as a result, business firms find themselves with stocks which are too high, the continued attempt to disinvest will force income below the equilibrium level. As a result a cyclical pattern somewhat similar to that in Table 2 ensues. However, a more rapid reduction in output of consumer goods

TABLE 6

The Cessation of Planned Investment in Inventories

Monthly periods	I	P	N	C	G.N.P.	H
1	1,000	4,500	100	4,400	5,500	3,300
2	1,000	4,400	80	4,320	5,400	3,380
3	1,000	4,300	60	4,240	5,300	3,440

would prevent this unwanted accumulation of inventories and hence eliminate the ensuing cycle. Thus, if the output of consumer goods were immediately reduced to 4,000, no undesired accumulation of stocks would occur. It can be argued that if an unwanted accumulation began, a very rapid downward adjustment in production would soon follow. If, in fact, any long-continued accumulation of stocks occurs during a period of contraction, it would suggest that business firms are willing to let this occur.

Though it is often suggested that a cessation in inventory accumulation must necessarily lead to a decline in the production of consumption goods this is not strictly true. During a period in which production is rising, an accumulation of inventories will occur as long as the level of shipments (or consumption) rises more slowly. Only if production rises above the full employment level of consumption will a subsequent decline be inevitable. However, because inventories are also an offset to saving, an increase in other forms of capital expenditure will be necessary if the level of income is to be maintained when the accumulation of inventories tapers off and disappears. In Table 6 a decline in income necessarily followed the cessation of planned inventory accumulation because expenditures on plant and equipment (I) had been assumed constant. But if, in period 2 of this Table, these expenditures had increased to 1,125 the system could have remained in equilibrium and as compared with period 1 no decline in income or in the production of consumption goods need have occurred. This point is illustrated in Chart 1.

The assumptions followed in the chart correspond to those in Model 1. Total savings in each period amount to 20 per cent of the total gross national product and this is offset by investment in durable assets plus net investment in inventories. The net investment in inventories is equal to the difference between the production of consumer goods and consumers' expenditures. When production tapers off smoothly at a full employment level, no decline in the output of consumer goods need occur provided there is a concurrent rise in investment in durable assets. This shift from one form of investment to another might occur almost automatically where firms are financing investment out of retained earnings and depreciation allowances. Once their need for financing further additions to inventory ceased they might immediately use the funds for other forms of investment. However, if production of consumer goods does go beyond this level, illustrated by the dotted line, a subsequent decline in the production of these goods is inevitable once the inventory accumulation ceases. In addition an even sharper rise in other forms of capital expenditure would be required if a decline in the level of income is to be avoided.

CHART 1

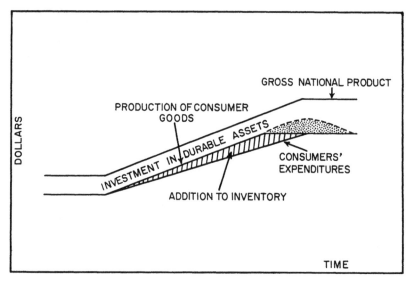

Investment in Inventories

Turning now to an analysis of a decline in income, let us assume that business firms attempt to reduce their stocks by 100 in each period. Table 7 shows that

TABLE 7

Planned Disinvestment in Inventories

Period	I	P	N	C	G.N.P.
1	1,000	4,000	0	4,000	5,000
2	1,000	3,900	— 20	3,920	4,900
3	1,000	3,800	— 40	3,840	4,800
4	1,000	3,700	— 60	3,760	4,700
5	1,000	3,600	— 80	3,680	4,600
6	1,000	3,500	—100	3,600	4,500
7	1,000	3,600	— 80	3,680	4,600

this attempt to reduce inventories by a fixed amount per period causes a cyclical decline in income which continues until a level of income is reached where the planned reduction in inventories is realized. This will be reached when income declines sufficiently so that the reduction in planned savings exactly balances the planned disinvestment in inventories, or in other words when the lower level of savings equals planned investment including the planned disinvestment in stocks. Suppose that business firms, having reduced their stocks to the required level, now increase production to the level required to meet current sales. When they do this they find that their plans are disappointed and that a reduction in their stocks continues. If they attempt to avoid this by increasing their production in each period, a cumulative upswing in income and employment will develop. But the decline in inventories will continue until the original equilibrium level of income is reached again. Thus the cessation of a planned reduction in inventories will be followed by an expansion in income, but the disinvestment in inventories will continue until the higher equilibrium level of income is regained. A cyclical pattern similar to that discussed above will develop here if producers try to reach and maintain some definite level of inventories. Here again the equilibrium level for both income and stocks would be reached more rapidly if producers adjusted their output more quickly.

The fact that the cessation of planned inventory liquidation leads automatically to an increase in production and employment is an important point. The effect is similar to that of a net increase in investment expenditures in stimulating a rise in income and this may help to explain how the lower turning point in a cyclical development leads directly into a cyclical upswing. Furthermore, a stimulating influence will develop as soon as business firms plan a reduction in their rate of liquidating inventory.[14] There need not be a complete cessation. It should be noted, however, that these conclusions are based on the assumption that the level of other forms of investment (I) and the propensity to consume are unchanged. For it is quite possible to apply the conclusion reached in Chart 1 to a period of inventory liquidation during a contraction. Thus the rate of liquidation might taper off and cease without any increase in production and employment if this stimulating influence were offset by a decline in other investment expenditures.

The arithmetic example given in Table 7 illustrates, in part, the independent role which an attempt to liquidate inventories may play in causing a cyclical contraction and resultant loss of income. Suppose the situation in period 1 represents equilibrium at full employment. Then assume that business firms fearing a business recession attempt to reduce their stocks. This produces the cyclical contraction in income shown in Table 7. Fear of recession, however much unfounded, will have produced a substantial loss of potential income. If other forms of investment continue unchanged business men will eventually find their stocks depleted and will cease their planned reduction in stocks. As a result income will gradually return to its full employment level. Meanwhile the reduction in stocks wil have continued. Business firms will find themselves back at the former income level with substantially less inventory on hand. If their stocks were initially appropriate to a full employment level they will now be too small. They can only restore them by diverting production either from other forms of investment or from consumption. This might be accompanied by inflation. It seems clear that anything that can be done to prevent this form of inventory recession with its resultant loss of income is highly desirable.

On the other hand when the liquidation of stocks takes place during a general contraction, a contraction accompanied by a substantial decline in other forms of investment, and when a subsequent accumulation of stocks accompanies a general expansion, the undesirability of this decline and rise in stocks is less evident. It can be argued that the loss of income which accompanies the contraction will be offset by the gain in income stimulated during the expansion, that over the cycle as a whole the net effect of inventory investment, aside from any gradual increase in stocks, will have been nil. This argument neglects the possibility that the attempt to reduce stocks may react unfavourably on other forms of investment, and hence may cause declines in activity which would not otherwise have occurred. In general, there seems reason to believe that anything that can be done to stabilize the level of inventories will contribute both to stabilizing the business cycle and to maintaining a higher average level of employment and income.

It is possible to combine in one model a planned increase both in investment in plant and equipment and investment in inventories. An illustration of this is given in Table 8.

TABLE 8

Investment in Inventories with a Concurrent Rise in the Level of Investment

in Plant and Equipment

Period	I	P	N	C	G.N.P.
1	1,000	4,000	0	4,000	5,000
2 (a)	1,100	4,100	—60	4,160	5,200
2 (b)	1,050	4,100	—20	4,120	5,150
2 (c)	1,025	4,100	0	4,100	5,125

Here business firms plan to increase their investment in inventories by 100 per period and at the same time increase their expenditures for durable assets to a level 100 higher than in period 1, illustrated by 2 (a), or alternatively to a level 50 higher than in period 2, illustrated by 2 (b), or 25 higher illustrated by 2 (c). Under the conditions in 2 (a) a decline in stocks will occur at first instead of the planned increase. In fact, no increase in stocks can occur until the increase in the production of consumer goods creates a level of income at which planned savings exceed the higher level of planned investment in durable assets. Thus a planned accumulation in stocks is more difficult to achieve if the investment in durable assets is rising concurrently. Similar conclusions hold with regard to a reduction in stocks. If investment expenditures for durable assets are falling, a planned reduction in stocks can be achieved only by a larger reduction in the production of goods for consumption than would be required if investment expenditures were stable.

By way of summary it would be useful to compare the conclusions reached in this simplified model with the views outlined in the previous chapter. One of the most important conclusions concerns the conditions under which an accumulation or reduction in inventories will take place. If the equilibrium level of income is defined as the income level where planned investment in plant and equipment is equal to planned savings, then, no accumulation in inventories will occur until income rises above this level. Furthermore, whenever income falls below this level inventories will decline. The more rapidly investment in plant and equipment increases, the more rapidly production of consumer goods must increase in order to achieve a planned investment in inventories. As was pointed out above, a conclusion similar to this is implicit in Mr. Hawtrey's theory. At a later stage of the argument, when a number of assumptions have been dropped, a conclusion even closer to that of Mr. Hawtrey will be reached.

It was shown that either as a result of an increased investment in plant and equipment or because of a planned investment in inventories a damped cyclical movement in income and employment can develop. The moving force in this cycle, which is essentially involuntary in nature, is the effort of business firms to restore their inventories to a satisfactory level. Moreover, if it is assumed that business firms expect all or some proportion of the increase in sales in the preceding period to be repeated, the cycle develops a greater amplitude and can become explosive if the coefficient of expectations and the marginal propensity to consume are both close to one.

Both the pattern of investment in inventories and the behaviour of total inventories in this involuntary cycle are consistent with the findings of Abramovitz about the movement of manufacturing inventories. However, planned as distinct from realized investment in inventories shows a lead in this model suggesting that the continued rise in investment in inventories right up to the peak of the cycle and its continued fall to the trough could be accounted for by involuntary changes. Similarly, the continued rise in total inventories after the peak of the cycle and the continued fall after the trough has been reached might reflect involuntary accumulations and decumulations.

While an involuntary cycle was shown to be a possible result, it is by no means a necessary result. Business firms can avoid unwanted accumulations in stocks by cutting back their output more rapidly than is assumed in the case of the model of an involuntary cycle. The same is true of undesired reductions in stocks. These can be avoided entirely if production of consumer goods increases immediately to the level of consumer spending corresponding to the higher equilibrium level of income.

It was also shown that a minor recession could result simply from the attempt of business firms to reduce their level of inventories. If investment in plant and equipment continues at its former level in spite of this planned reduction in stocks, income will move back to its former equilibrium level as soon as the business firms discontinue their efforts to liquidate inventories. But business firms will find themselves back at their former sales position with smaller stocks than before. If these are now inadequate they can only be restored by a further increase in production. If the initial equilibrium position was one of full employment this might prove inflationary.

In terms of our simple model it was also possible to show that changes in the level of planned investment in inventories might be an important factor in leading to a downturn or in initiating revival. The cessation of a planned disinvestment in stocks or a reduction in the rate of disinvestment will lead automatically to an increase in income and employment if other investment expenditures do not decline further. This initial upward movement could be the start of a general period of expansion if it, in turn, caused other investment expenditure to increase. Similarly, a cessation of planned investment in inventories or a slowing up in its rate could precipitate a downturn, for it would cause income to fall unless offset by an increase in other forms of expenditure. On the other hand, if expenditures for plant and equipment are increasing at the time that planned investment in inventories begins to fall off, there may be no fall in the level of income and even the rate of production in those industries that had been producing goods for inventory may not decline.

Finally the model indicated that investment in inventories is likely to be an important factor reinforcing both the expansion and contraction phases of the major cycle. It was shown that if business firms wish to avoid unwanted reductions in stocks on the upswing and unwanted accumulations on the downswing they will find it necessary to increase and decrease their production rapidly relative to the rate at which investment in plant and equipment is changing. Whether the disinvestment and reinvestment in inventories that occurs during a major depression causes any net loss of income will depend on the importance of its indirect effects. As far as the direct effects are concerned, it can be argued that the loss of income caused by disinvestment during the contraction is counterbalanced by the addition to income resulting from reinvestment during the upswing.

CHAPTER FOUR

A SECOND MODEL

THE RESULTS OBTAINED in the first model are partially modified when the assumption regarding the timing of the receipt and expenditure of income is changed. In Model 1 it was assumed that all income was paid out in the period in which it was earned and expenditures were made out of it in the same period. This is just the reverse of the assumption made in the Robertsonian form of period analysis where it is assumed that income earned in one period is not spent until the following period. It is now desirable to examine this assumption more carefully.

During any period of time, changes in expenditure may precede, coincide with, or lag behind changes in the receipt of income. The relative timing of different expenditures varies with the type of income with reference which it is made, and with the availability and habits in the use of credit. To discover the true relationship, separate consideration must be given to the receipt and expenditure out of such different types of income as salaries and wages, income of unincorporated enterprise, and corporate income. The net expenditure during any period will be the total of expenditures made from these various forms of income and of expenditures financed by credit. In the following paragraphs an attempt is made to gather together whatever evidence is available on the relative proportions of these different forms of income in the Canadian economy and on the way in which any increase or decrease in such income is likely to affect expenditures.

In the Canadian economy wage earners are paid primarily on a weekly basis while salaried workers are paid on a monthly or semi-monthly basis. Though no direct evidence is available on how soon an increase in salaries or wages will result in increased expenditures, it seems reasonable to expect that it will have its major effects on expenditures within the month in which it is paid. Some difference might occur depending on the extent to which the increase represented higher wage rates or increased employment; a greater lag between income and expenditure might be expected in the former case. There is also some support for the belief that spending habits adjust themselves somewhat slowly to changes in income, that a rapid increase in income results only in a gradually rising level of expenditure, and similarly that when incomes decline individuals attempt to maintain their standard of living.[1] This would lead one to expect a somewhat higher proportion of saving during an upswing and a falling off in the proportion of income saved during a period of recession. For Model 2 it will be assumed that any increase in wages affects spending entirely in the month in which it is received. Some lag between wage income and expenditure may exist but it seems likely that it will be sufficiently unimportant to justify neglecting it entirely. Wage earners ordinarily spend almost their entire income and they have little backlog of savings to draw on when they suffer a decline in income.

Though salaries differ somewhat from wages in regard to the time of their receipt and expenditure, the difference is not great. The actual funds of employees receiving a monthly salary will not be available for expenditure until the following month, but some increase in expenditures could be expected by individuals who use up their savings or spend on credit in anticipation of the actual income receipt. Lack of credit or savings would place some limits on this type of spending and for this reason some lag could be expected. The difference between salaries and wages would be correspondingly smaller where salaries are paid more than once a month. It will be assumed here that salaried income is also spent within the month in which it is earned. The possible lag will be taken care of under the income of unincorporated enterprise.

Income of unincorporated enterprises is subject to more uncertainty than salary and wage income and for this reason there may be a greater lag between any increase in income and the resulting increase in expenditure. Seasonal variations and irregular factors frequently tend to make it more difficult for the individuals concerned to gauge the extent of any increase in income until some time has elapsed. For this reason it will be assumed that incomes of this type will only result in increased expenditure with a lag of one month.

A much longer lag exists between the time corporate income is earned and the time it affects consumers' spending. This difference centres around the dividend policies of corporations. Examination of annual information for Canada and United States offers some evidence that an increase in corporate income is often reflected in higher dividend payments in the following year. This may reflect the fact that increased dividend rates and extra dividends are often announced at the time of the corporation's annual statement. The largest proportion of these occur during the first quarter of the calendar year. In addition to this, reserves of income are accumulated during periods of prosperity and these are used to maintain dividends on preferred stocks and on common stocks of the better established companies during periods of depressed earnings. Thus in Canada during the period 1926 to 1929 only about one-half of corporate earnings after tax were paid out as dividends, while between 1930 and 1935 payments of dividends exceeded earnings by 25 per cent. Similarly during the war period 1940 to 1945 only slightly over one-half corporate earnings after tax were paid out as dividends, and during the post-war period 1946 to 1950 corporations retained from 50 to 60 per cent of their earnings after tax.

The reasons for this pattern will not be examined here; it apparently reflects both the structure of corporate financing and rather strong financial traditions. However, even when income is not paid out as dividends, individuals may increase their expenditures by realizing capital gains, and in the past this has been an important factor though its influence does not seem to be large at the present time. It is assumed in the present model that increases or decreases in corporate income do not result in increased or decreased expenditures by individuals until a year or more after their occurrence. Though no evidence is available on the effects of the receipt of dividends upon consumers' expenditures it seems reasonable to believe that the propensity to spend this type of income will be low.[2] Because of this the conclusions reached in this chapter are not substantially changed whether corporate income is paid out as dividends or not.

The use of consumer credit exerts some influence on the relation between personal income and expenditure. During an upswing its use, whether in the form of instalment buying or charge accounts, will allow some purchases to be made in advance of the receipt of income. Similarly, during a contraction, repayment of outstanding accounts may cause expenditures to fall off more rapidly than they otherwise would. The year-to-year increase in the amount of consumer credit outstanding in the period 1946 to 1950 in Canada, compared with the corresponding increase in total consumer expenditure, averaged 19 per cent with a variation from 13 to 33 per cent in individual years.[3] Undoubtedly these data are unusually high both because the use of consumer credit had been curtailed during the war and because the period from 1946 to 1950 was one in which consumers' buying of durables was very heavy. Data for an earlier period in the United States indicate a somewhat lower ratio. Thus in the period 1929 to 1941 the change in the amount of consumer credit outstanding averaged 11 per cent of the corresponding change in consumer expenditure during years of contraction and 16 per cent during years of expansion.[4] In the period as a whole it averaged 13.6 per cent. On a month-to-month basis it is difficult to determine the exact effects of this on the time sequence between expenditures and incomes. In general, it can be argued that the consumers' use of credit would tend to reduce the lag between the receipt of income and its subsequent expenditure. Rather than introduce credit separately into our model its effects will be subsumed by showing a high rate of spending out of salary and wage income within the month in which it is earned.

Thus in Model 2 it will be assumed that any spending out of salaries and wages occurs during the month in which the income is earned; spending out of earnings of unincorporated enterprise occurs with a lag of one month; and consumers' spending out of corporate profits occurs only when the dividends are paid or roughly a year after the income is earned. It is also necessary to make some assumptions regarding the proportion of incomes falling into each of these

TABLE 9

The Share of Different Types of Income in Changes in Gross National Product, Canada, 1926 to 1950

	Salaries and wages	Corporate profits before tax	Farm income	Unincorporated, non-farm income
	Per cent			
1926—29	65.5	14.6	x	10.6
1929—33	44.0	15.4	12.8	12.0
1933—37	41.0	25.6	12.0	8.8
1937—38	19.7	74.5	x	0.0
1938—41	44.5	18.5	4.0	5.3
1946—50	45.8	14.1	7.9	7.1
1929—32	40.2	21.4	12.5	11.0
1932—37	35.0	36.1	11.5	6.7
1926—28	42.8	15.7	4.4	8.4
1928—33	36.2	16.1	22.8	11.4

x indicates that the two totals moved in opposite directions.

SOURCE: Canada, Dominion Bureau of Statistics, *National Accounts: Income and Expenditure, 1926—1950* (Ottawa, 1952).

categories, and to distinguish between the marginal and average amounts of incomes going to each group, since the former fluctuate considerably.

Table 9 sets forth the extent to which each of the three main types of income share in an increase or decrease in total gross national product. Data are presented for each period of expansion and contraction, the war years excepted, from 1926 to 1950. Because farm income reached a peak in 1928 and corporate profits a trough in 1932 data are also presented for the periods 1926 to 1928 and 1928 to 1933 and for the periods 1929 to 1932 and 1932 to 1937. The figures in each case show the increase or decrease in the particular form of income expressed as a percentage of the corresponding increase or decrease in gross national product for the period in question. As a basis of comparison for these marginal changes it should be kept in mind that during this period the average share of each of these forms of income in the gross national product over the period 1926 to 1950 was as follows: salaries and wages, 47.5 per cent; corporate income, 9.5 per cent; farm income, 7.9 per cent; and income of unincorporated enterprise (excluding farm income), 8.2 per cent.

The marginal relationship for salaries and wages though more variable than the average relation does not differ markedly from it. Thus an examination of the data given in Table 9 indicates that it would be reasonable to assume that about 45 or 50 per cent of any increase or decrease in the gross national product goes to salaries and wages. A greater difference between marginal and average relationships is indicated for income of unincorporated enterprises, primarily on account of the variability of farm income. Thus in comparison with an average share in gross national product of 16 per cent, the marginal relation for this type of income has varied from about 0 to 34 per cent. Corporate income also shows a wide variation: whereas the average share of corporate income is only about 9 per cent, the year-to-year changes in corporate income frequently amount to 20 per cent or more of the corresponding change in gross national product. Further, there is some evidence that this marginal relationship for corporate income is especially large in years which are turning points in a business cycle. The data included in Table 9 are, of course, drawn from a world in which prices change, often by large amounts. In incorporating assumptions based on these data into our present model, which specifically assumes no price changes, there is some inconsistency. However, when the present model is subsequently modified to include the effects of price changes, this inconsistency will disappear. In the meantime this limitation should be kept in mind.

On the basis of the foregoing discussions the following assumptions are adopted for Model 2: 50 per cent of any increase in income is paid out in the form of salaries and wages and 90 per cent of this is spent within the same period; 25 per cent of any increase in income goes into corporate profits and 40 per cent of this is paid out with a lag of one year; the remaining 25 per cent of each increase in income goes into income of independent enterprises and this results in increased expenditures in the following period amounting to 80 per cent of the increase.

If the example of Table 2 is now analysed in terms of this second model the results are substantially modified as is shown by Table 10. In this instance manufacturers attempt to produce sufficient to meet the sales of the preceding period and replace the inventory loss that has occurred. It is apparent that the cyclical pattern in the level of gross national product, while still present, is much

TABLE 10

An Inventory Cycle with Expenditure Lags

Period	I	P	N	C	G.N.P.	H	Np
1	1,000	4,000	0	4,000	5,000	3,000	0
2	1,100	4,000	—45	4,045	5,100	2,955	0
3	1,100	4,090	—15	4,105	5,190	2,940	45
4	1,100	4,165	8	4,157	5,265	2,948	60
5	1,100	4,209	17	4,192	5,309	2,965	52
6	1,100	4,227	18	4,209	5,327	2,983	35
7	1,100	4,226	13	4,213	5,326	2,996	17
8	1,100	4,217	8	4,209	5,317	3,004	4
9	1,100	4,205	3	4,202	5,305	3,007	—4
10	1,100	4,195	— 1	4,196	5,295	3,006	—7
11	1,100	4,190	— 3	4,193	5,290	3,003	—6
12	1,100	4,190	— 2	4,192	5,290	3,001	—3

I—Investment in plant and equipment; P—Production of consumer goods; N—Net change in inventories; C—Consumers' expenditures; G.N.P.—Total income $= P + I = I + N + C$; H—Total inventories; Np—Planned investment in inventories.

smaller in amplitude than for the corresponding table in the first model Table 2, and an equilibrium is approached much more quickly.

Because the over-all propensity to consume is smaller, the equilibrium level of income is lower than in the first model. As long as income is rising uniformly and before the effects of the lag in spending out of corporate dividends become effective, the marginal propensity to consume is 65 per cent. This corresponds to a multiplier of about 2.86. However, in Table 10, where the change in income from period to period varies, the size of the short-run marginal propensity to consume will fluctuate because of the lag in expenditures. By the short-run marginal propensity to consume is meant the increase in consumption in that period divided by the increase in income in the same period.

As Professor Metzler has pointed out, the effect of a lower marginal propensity to consume is to make the inventory cycles shorter in duration and more highly damped.[5] The cycle develops, as we saw, because the attempt to restore an initial decline in inventories is partially self-defeating. Each increase in production for inventories leads to a further increase in sales which partially prevents the planned increase in inventories from taking place. The lower the marginal propensity to consume, the smaller will be the increase in sales resulting from each increase in output and the more easily will the initial reduction in inventories be restored. If, as there seems good reason to believe, the over-all marginal propensity to consume is somewhere in the neighbourhood of two-thirds, the inventory cycle will be more damped and shorter than appeared in our first model.

The partial lag in expenditure behind income also has an effect on the cycle. Because of it the initial decline in inventories is smaller and the ensuing cycle is more highly damped and of slightly longer duration. The amplitude of the cycle is smaller both because the initial decline in inventories is reduced by the lag in expenditure and because, once the level of income begins to decline, this lag keeps sales from declining as rapidly as they would in a model not considering it, which in turn reduces undesired inventory accumulations. These same factors lengthen the cycle slightly.

In Table 10 it was assumed that increased investment preceded the rise in the production of consumer goods and that subsequently producers followed an automatic rule of attempting to meet last month's sales plus the loss in inventory. Both of these assumptions are unnecessarily unrealistic. There is no evidence that capital expenditures or, more generally, activity in the capital goods industries, precedes production of consumption goods on either the upswing or downswing. On the contrary, there is some reason for expecting a lag in capital expenditures in the downswing. Much capital equipment is produced on binding orders and these orders will be completed even though new orders drop off sharply. Moreover, construction projects which are underway often take some time to finish, thus causing fluctuations in actual expenditures to lag behind new orders. Nor are actual changes in inventories known as accurately as is assumed in Table 10. Seasonal and irregular factors may often make it difficult for the business man to determine whether there is a cyclical upswing or downswing in either sales or inventories.[6] Furthermore, all inventories are not located in one place as is tacitly assumed in the above model. An increase in consumers' expenditures may be spread unevenly among types of commodities, types of stores, and areas. The resulting decline in inventories in retail stores affects the manufacturer, but only indirectly, through the new orders he receives. In view of these uncertainties it seems more probable that business men will adopt a rule-of-thumb procedure such as increasing their production at a certain rate when their anticipations improve or when they see their sales increasing. For these reasons, in Table 11 it will be assumed that the production of consumer

TABLE 11

An Inventory Sequence with Investment and Production of

Consumer Goods Rising Concurrently

Monthly period	I	P	N	C	G.N.P.	H
1	1,000	4,000	0	4,000	5,000	3,000
2	1,100	4,050	—17	4,067	5,150	2,983
3	1,100	4,100	—20	4,120	5,200	2,963
4	1,100	4,150	— 2	4,152	5,250	2,061
5	1,100	4,200	15	4,185	5,300	2,976
6	1,100	4,250	33	4,217	5,350	3,009
7	1,100	4,200	— 5	4,205	5,300	3,004
8	1,100	4,200	5	4,195	5,300	3,009

goods begins to rise simultaneously with that of capital goods (there is a general growth business confidence) and that business men increase their production of consumer goods by a constant amount each period, namely, by 50. In this example, there is still an initial decline in stocks but this only lasts a short time. In the fifth month stocks begin to rise and if the rise in production continues it will soon be discouraged by a fairly rapid accumulation of stocks. Thus unless entrepreneurs wish to build up their stocks, production will soon be stabilized at or about the higher equilibrium level.

The assumption that capital expenditures rise suddenly to a higher level is also unrealistic. Examination of annual changes in capital expenditures indicates that the rate of change each month is rarely more than 3 per cent and the average is about 2 per cent. In Table 12 it is assumed that instead of a sudden rise of

TABLE 12

An Inventory Sequence with Investment Rising Slowly

Monthly period	I	P	N	C	G.N.P.	H
1	1,000	4,000	0	4,000	5,000	3,000
2	1,020	4,050	18	4,032	5,070	3,018
3	1,040	4,100	23	4,077	5,210	3,041
4	1,060	4,150	27	4,123	5,210	3,068
5	1,080	4,200	32	4,168	5,280	3,100
6	1,100	4,200	9	4,191	5,300	3,109
7	1,100	4,200	5	4,195	5,300	3,114

capital expenditures to 1,100 in period 2, there is a gradual increase of 20 per period. All other assumptions remain the same. In this example the initial decline in inventories disappears; instead, some accumulation of stocks accompanies the rise in income and the higher level of income is reached without any appreciable cyclical effect. The amount of inventory accumulation depends in part on how rapidly the increase in production of consumer goods occurs. Practically no accumulation would occur if production increased by 40 each period; a larger increase than this in each period would cause some accumulation. The dividing line depends on the size of the multiplier which is determined by the short-period marginal propensity to consume. Given a constant lag this marginal propensity to consume will be constant as long as income rises at a uniform rate. Inventories will accumulate whenever production increases rapidly enough to cause income to exceed the equilibrium level determined by the short-run marginal propensity to consume. In the initial stages before the lag in expenditure becomes effective this propensity will be smaller and inventories can be accumulated more readily. The lag in expenditure will exert an opposite effect at the stage where expenditures level off or turn down, and cause some reduction in inventories or make the accumulation somewhat smaller. These conclusions apply even though there are lags of different lengths and investment expenditures do not rise at a uniform rate. Inventories will accumulate whenever production rises sufficiently to cause income to exceed the equilibrium level determined by the short-run marginal propensity to consume. They will be reduced whenever it rises by less than that amount. However, when the rate of growth of income is changing, this propensity will vary from period to period, and the equilibrium level of income will vary with it.

In Metzler's models of the inventory cycle and in the models examined above it was assumed that investment rose by a given amount and then remained stable at this higher level. In actual fact inventory fluctuations take place against a more or less continuous expansion or contraction in investment expenditures. If the inventory cycle of Table 2 is re-examined in terms of a model where investment expenditures continue to increase in each period by a fixed amount of

20 units, the cycle becomes highly damped. In fact, even with a marginal propensity to consume as high as .8, the resulting cycle never causes any actual reduction in the level of income or in the output of consumer goods. The cycle merely shows up as a variation in the rate of increase in output and income.

When the effects of a planned accumulation of inventory are examined under the assumptions in the second model it becomes apparent that here too the results in the first model are modified. In Table 13, business men increase their production by 100 in each period, and continue to do so until they achieve an investment in inventories of about 100 per period. Expenditure lags and the size of the marginal propensity to consume is assumed to be the same as in Table 10.

TABLE 13

Planned Investment in Inventories with Lags in Expenditure

Monthly period	I	P	N	C	G.N.P.
1	1,000	4,000		4,000	5,000
2	1,000	4,100	55	4,145	5,100
3	1,000	4,200	90	4,110	5,200
4	1,000	4,300	125	4,175	5,300
5	1,000	4,300	105	4,195	5,300
6	1,000	4,200	50	4,150	5,200
7	1,000	4,100	15	4,085	5,100
8	1,000	4,000	— 20	4,020	5,000
9	1,000	4,000	0	4,000	5,000

A comparison of Table 13 with Table 5 indicates that the more realistic assumptions of the second model allow the planned accumulation of inventory to be realized much more rapidly. An accumulation of 100 each month is realized within three months whereas in Model 1 this level was reached only after six months. Because the multiplier is smaller, the higher accumulation of inventory is reached with a smaller rise in income. When this is accomplished and producers curtail their operations, some unplanned increases in stocks may occur. But the partial lag in the fall in expenditures results in a much smaller accumulation than occurred in the first model, and this could be avoided entirely by a more rapid reduction in production.

The assumption regarding the lag between income and expenditure adopted in this model represents the best guess at the actual state of affairs. If a larger share of income is subject to a lag or if the average lag is longer, the results will be modified accordingly. In both instances, the effect would be a lessening of the initial reduction in inventories resulting from an increase in investment expenditures or the fuller realisation from the start, of the planned accumulation of inventories. Because the initial increase in expenditure caused by any increase in production would be smaller, it would be easier to avoid any undesired accumulation or liquidation of inventories and any inventory cycles which still appeared would be more highly damped.

The rate at which capital expenditures change is a crucial factor both in determining the ability of business firms to accumulate or liquidate inventories and in governing the rate at which business activity may expand or contract. A rapid increase in the rate of capital expenditure will cause a depletion in inventories unless the production of consumers' goods is also increased rapidly. Similarly, a rapid decline in capital expenditures (on durable assets) will result in the accumulation of stocks unless production declines at a sufficiently rapid rate. If we define an equilibrium rate of change in the production of consumer goods as that which results in no change in the level of inventories, then this rate will vary directly with the rate of change in capital expenditures and with the size of the marginal propensity to consume. If manufacturers wish to reduce their stocks during a downswing they must decrease their production even more rapidly than this equilibrium rate. The reverse is true during an upswing.

It is important to remember that the analysis thus far has been in aggregative terms. If allowance is made for this the argument is reinforced. Not only are all manufacturers forced to add to their inventories if they increase their production too quickly but if any individual increases his production more rapidly than the average of all firms he is likely to be faced with an increase in stocks that is larger than average. Some allowance must of course be made for the fact that the demand for some products and even some firm's products will increase more rapidly than the average demand for all products. These firms can accordingly increase their production more rapidly without being faced with mounting stocks; but in the aggregate their experience will be offset by others who experience a smaller than average increase in demand. The general business climate is such an important factor in determining the rate at which an expansion (or contraction) is likely to proceed because all firms must move together.[7] When business men are optimistic all firms will increase their production simultaneously and if there is a concurrent increase in capital expenditures the level of business activity may move upward rapidly.

In the above discussion no attempt has been made to relate business men's decisions as to what they consider an appropriate level of stocks to the current level of sales. Professor Metzler has elaborated a model of this type using what he calls an accelerator to designate the ratio of stock to sales that business firms attempt to maintain.[8] His conclusion is that, except for relatively small values for the marginal propensity to consume and the accelerator, the system will be unstable. Thus if we let a stand for the accelerator and b stand for the marginal propensity to consume, the system will only be stable if $b (1 + a) < 1$. For values of that expression which exceed one, the system will at first oscillate in cycles of ever increasing amplitude and for still larger values will diverge steadily. Where the model becomes unstable some limits to fluctuations in production will be imposed by the fact that output cannot be reduced below zero in the downward direction and can be increased beyond the industry's capacity only to a limited extent in the upward direction.[9]

The evidence that business firms usually allow their ratio of stocks to sales to decline in periods of increasing sales and to increase during periods of falling sales makes the relevance of the unstable form of this model doubtful.[10] T. M. Whitin has argued that if business firms follow a rational inventory control policy they will vary their inventory in proportion to the square root of their sales rather than directly with total sales. Using this assumption he has shown that Metzler's unstable accelerator model becomes stable.[11] It seems clear that while some accelerative effect may be present, the size of the accelerator will usually be small. In the period of contraction and expansion from 1929 to 1937 the reduction and increase in total inventories in both Canada and the United States only amounted to one-fourth or less of the corresponding change in gross national product. If some of the change in inventory at the peaks and trough of this period was involuntary the desired change must have been even smaller in relation to the change in output.

In the models developed by Metzler the ratio of stocks to sales declines in the early stages of an expansion but rises well before the peak in sales and output is reached. Some of this difference between theoretical and observed results may be due to the fact that the inventory fluctuations in the model occur against the background of a single change in investment expenditures instead of the gradually rising or falling expenditures that ordinarily occurs. Moreover, the wide variations in the ratio that occur in practice would seem to suggest that the size of the inventory a firm carries in relation to its total sales is, in practice, quite flexible. Hence models which assume a rigid relation between the change in inventories in each period and the planned change in production in the following period are of questionable validity. Accordingly, some doubt is cast on the involuntary cycle of the Metzler type.

Nevertheless, the fact that firms may wish to hold larger inventories when the level of sales is higher is an important consideration. Even if it does not lead to involuntary oscillations as Metzler's model would suggest, it helps to explain why investment in inventories tends to reinforce major expansion and contraction in income. It has just been argued that the individual firm's ability to accumulate or reduce stocks will depend on the speed with which it adjusts its production relative to the change in capital investment. The importance of the acceleration effect will depend on how quickly firms wish to restore inventories to what they consider a normal position and, as will be argued below, on the extent to which they increase prices to defend inventory positions or cut them to clear surplus stocks.

No attempt has been made in the above examples to show the effects of the lag in payment of corporate profits. The effects in each case would depend on whether these increased income payments tended to reinforce or offset the other tendencies present at the time they became effective. Very little is known about the extent to which income in the form of dividends is spent on consumer goods. In general, dividends are received by individuals in the higher income groups and hence the propensity to consume out of this form of income may be low. Evidence of two types of lags has been mentioned: one of about a year and a much longer lag in which income earned during a boom period is paid out in an ensuing depression. It might be argued that this latter lag exercises a stabilizing effect on the level of income by decreasing consumers' spending during a boom period and increasing it during a depression. However, this argument is of doubtful validity because the undistributed profits of the boom period are often spent by the firm on capital goods almost as soon as they are earned.

In the second model the principal modification of our previous conclusions concerns the level of income which must be exceeded before an accumulation of stocks will occur. In the first model where there were no lags in expenditure. this income level was the equilibrium level as determined by the schedules of saving and investment. With lags in expenditure, however, the relevant income level is the equilibrium level as determined by the short-run marginal propensity to consume, and it may be above, below, or identical with the corresponding equilibrium income level of Model 1. It will usually be below at the beginning of an expansion and an accumulation of stocks can be achieved somewhat more easily as a result; it will ordinarily be above at the onset of a contraction and as a result a reduction in stocks can be achieved more readily.

A number of considerations advanced in this chapter cast further doubt on the argument that there is an involuntary inventory cycle caused by the continual attempt of business firms to reach a satisfactory inventory position. When there is some lag in consumers' spending, an increase in investment expenditures is less likely to cause an involuntary decline in stocks. Evidence was also advanced to indicate that during periods of cyclical contraction and expansion, such as those that occurred in the 1930's, the over-all marginal propensity to save is likely to be fairly large. This also tends to make it easier for business firms to avoid unwanted reductions in inventories and to restore inventories to a satisfactory position. Such a conclusion is reinforced by the fact that investment expenditures ordinarily increase at a moderate rate and may often lag behind production of consumer goods because of the long time required for planning investment projects and the length of time required for completing projects already underway. All of these considerations suggest that business firms can avoid a continued accumulation or liquidation of inventories provided they are willing to make sufficiently sharp adjustments in production. It would also suggest that when stocks accumulate in the face of declining sales or decline during a period of increasing sales it must be for some reason other than the mere inability to avoid it. This conclusion does not hold where output cannot be readily changed—where the short-run supply schedule is quite inelastic. In other respects the conclusions reached in the preceding chapter remain substantially unchanged.

CHAPTER FIVE

THE EFFECTS OF INVENTORY FLUCTUATIONS ON
DIFFERENT COMMODITIES
AND STAGES OF PRODUCTION

A BASIC CONCLUSION which emerged from the preceding analysis is that an accumulation or liquidation of inventories can only occur when the production of consumer goods is respectively above or below the level which is appropriate to the equilibrium level of income as previously defined. This is subject to qualification to the extent that lags in expenditure out of income are present. But this conclusion takes no account of possible variations which may occur within total inventories, for it is consistent with the above conclusion that an accumulation might occur in respect to one class of inventories, which was exactly offset by the decline in another type of inventory, the total volume of inventories remaining unchanged. It is the purpose of this chapter to examine in some detail the extent to which consideration of the behaviour of different types of inventory affects our previous analysis.

Inventories of different types of goods may be expected to react differently at various stages of the cycle. Certain well-established facts regarding the business cycle suggest the following basis of analysis: inventories can be classified according to the type of goods held, according to the type of holder, and according to the stage of fabrication. Considerations both of demand and supply enter into this classification. On the question of demand, it has long been known that the production of durable goods, notably producers' durables and construction materials, tends to decline to a greater extent during a contraction than the production of less durable goods. A detailed study of this problem has revealed that, although durability bears a fairly close positive correlation to the degree of fluctuation in demand throughout the business cycle, it is by no means the sole determinant. A number of commodities which are ordinarily considered less durable, such as flowers, sports equipment, and tools, also showed a very sharp decline in production during the depression of the 1930's. In some respects, a direct classification according to income elasticity might be the most useful basis for distinguishing the degree to which various goods are subject to cyclical fluctuations in demand and production.[1]

From the standpoint of supply, the more stable character of agricultural production throughout periods of prosperity and depression is well established. Thus a world index of agricultural production continued almost unchanged from 1929 to 1933 whereas an index of non-agricultural primary production fell from 114 in 1929 to 75 in 1932 and an index of industrial production (mining and manufacturing) for the world excluding the U.S.S.R. declined from 100 to 63 over this same period. In this latter instance the contrast between durable and non-durable goods was especially marked.[2] Since agricultural production (except for fluctuations of a climatic nature continues almost unchanged throughout most periods of business depression it is not surprising that consumption of these commodities declines more than production at such a time so that an accumulation of stocks results. Thus a world index of stocks of agricultural primary products (on a base 1925-9 = 100) increased from 117.1 in 1929 to 153 in 1933; by the first quarter of 1937 it had declined to 116.5.[3] Although unusually severe droughts contributed to the latter decline, it also reflected the increased rate of consumption as the world recovered from the depression. The counter-cyclical fluctuation in stocks of primary agricultural products is reduced because the consumption of many products using agricultural raw materials and foodstuffs declines to only a moderate extent in depressed periods and the unusually low prices which accompany the accumulation of stocks encourage the maintenance of consumption. There is, of course, some difference in the degree to which the consumption of different agricultural products varies. Probably the largest stock accumulations are of hides and wool which are by-products of the output of foodstuffs, for which demand declines least of all.[4] This statement is supported by data on world stocks: an index of stocks of agricultural raw materials (excluding foodstuffs) showed a larger increase between 1929 and 1933 than an index of stocks of foodstuffs. The former index increased from 106.4 in 1929 to 155.5 in 1933 whereas the latter increased from 122.6 to 151.7 over this same period.[5]

However, the accumulation of stocks of primary products was not confined to agricultural commodities. A world index of stocks of non-agricultural primary products, which includes rubber, petroleum, iron ore, copper, lead, zinc, tin, and cement, also showed a substantial rise in the depression of the 1930's. Consumption of these commodities also fell off more rapidly than production although the causes are not so readily apparent. Many of these commodities are used in the production of more durable goods, both consumers' and producers', demand for which declines most sharply during a recession. An equally sharp decline in the production of these industrial materials would have been necessary in order to avoid such an accumulation of inventories. Rubber is like an agricultural commodity in that its production cannot easily be reduced in periods of slack demand. Competitive exploitation of a common pool sometimes prevents any substantial decline in the production of petroleum. In some instances international cartels which attempted to maintain prices by holding stocks off the market may have contributed to the rise in world stocks of these non-agricultural commodities.

While a more rapid decline in consumption than in production will give rise to an accumulation of stocks, it does not immediately determine the stage at which this accumulation will take place. Thus, while it is evident that a falling off in purchases of clothing during a period when the production of such items as cotton and wool are well maintained will lead to some accumulation of cotton and wool, it does not tell us at what stage of production this will occur. A number of factors must be considered in attempting to analyse this problem and in general they tend to indicate that accumulation occurs at the primary level.

Primary commodities are usually standardized, easily stored, and unspecialized. In contrast, the more highly fabricated any commodity becomes the more specialized and limited the market becomes and the more subject it is to obsolescence. Thus, in the above example, stocks would never be kept in the form of women's clothing for more than a short period of time because of the risk inherent in frequent changes in style. While this is an extreme case, it is in some degree true of a wide range of finished commodities. Further, the more highly fabricated the commodity, the larger the investment tied up in it. Both the cost and availability of investment funds may be factors limiting investment in more finished materials. On the other hand they are sometimes more compact and easily stored than primary products. In any case the cost of storage is a smaller percentage of the value of the commodity in its finished form and if, as is frequently the case during a depression, the manufacturer or distributor has extra space in his warehouse the storage cost is very small. The higher cost of insurance and the larger amount of interest which must be paid to finance the inventory of more expensive finished goods would be offsetting factors.

The risk of changes in price is also an important reason why stocks of goods may tend to accumulate in the form of primary commodities. Many primary commodities are bought and sold on highly organized speculative markets and the manufacturer or dealer can pass the risk of changes in price on to professional speculators.[6] This is not possible with more highly manufactured articles. Since periods of declining consumption are also usually periods of falling prices, manufacturers and distributors will be reluctant to hold any stocks in excess of the minimum requirements because of the loss they may incur on further price declines. However, if stocks are accumulating because manufacturers have failed to reduce production in relation to falling consumption, it may indicate that they prefer to hold these stocks rather than attempt to sell them off by reducing prices or cut back production even more sharply. A certain reluctance to follow either course may arise from a fear of spoiling the market and a feeling of obligation towards the firm's older employees. On the other hand, after both prices and wages have fallen sharply for some time one might suppose that manufacturers would have an incentive to purchase raw materials and to use their idle plant and the plentiful supply of skilled labour to fabricate them into at least a semi-finished stage, for example, steel sheets, finished leather, or cloth. Where firms have both idle storage space and idle funds the cost of such an operation would be minimized. This, of course, may be one of the factors which operates to bring a period of depressed activity to an end.

Another factor which affects the stage at which inventories tend to accumulate is the structure of orders throughout industry. When goods are purchased under binding orders at certain stages of production, some firms will be forced to accept materials under order for some time after their own sales have begun to fall off. This would be true wherever sales under binding orders did not carry through to the purchaser of the final product, as it rarely does in the case of consumer goods. Very little is known about the structure of orders, however, and until more detailed information is available no definite conclusions are possible regarding the effect this may have on inventory accumulation.

When the initial decline in activity occurs as a result of a lessening of demand at the retail level, perhaps owing to an increased rate of saving or a reduction in investment activity, one of the first signs of this decline will be some accumulation of stocks in retail channels. Provided their orders are subject to cancellation, retailers can attempt to avoid any further accumulation and can actually reduce their stocks by cutting down their new purchases sufficiently sharply. Manufacturers, in turn faced with falling orders, can attempt to avoid any accumulation of stocks by cutting down on the new production they undertake. For technical reasons (for example, the necessity of closing down a whole assembly line at one time), manufacturers may find themselves in a slightly less flexible position than retailers. But provided they in turn can cancel outstanding orders, the manufacturers can cut down on their purchases of new materials and can gradually reduce the scale of their productive operations.

Although producers and distributors at each stage may attempt to avoid an accumulation of stocks by a sufficiently sharp reduction in their own purchases, a net reduction in stocks may or may not be achieved in the economy as a whole. According to the argument developed above, a net reduction of stocks will only be achieved if the production of consumer goods is reduced below the level appropriate to the equilibrium level of income determined by the rate of activity in the investment goods industry and the community's propensity to save. Lags in consumers' spending will also make it easier ot achieve a reduction of stocks. Since there is some evidence that investment expenditures decline with a lag during the early stages of a recession it would seem probable that retailers and manufacturers should be able to achieve some net reduction in stocks at that time. But if individuals attempt to increase their rate of saving at this time, in order to build up a reserve lest they too become unemployed, the equilibrium level of income might fall rapidly making a reduction of stocks difficult to achieve. In such circumstances very sharp cuts in new purchases on the part of the retailer and marked reductions in new production and new purchases on the part of the manufacturer may be required to achieve a reduction in stocks. This does not mean, of course, that manufacturers or retailers will in all cases attempt to reduce their stocks.

A somewhat similar situation exists during a period of recovery. If the initial increase in demand arises from incomes induced by increased investment expenditures or government public works expenditures, the first result of the increased demand for goods will be a decline in stocks held by retailers. Retailers will in turn increase their orders from the manufacturer and these orders will be filled from the manufacturer's inventory of finished goods. The manufacturer, in turn, will attempt to increase his rate of production but whether he will be in a position to do so or not will depend on the adequacy of his inventory of raw materials. Evidence has been presented that inventories of a number of primary unfabricated commodities move in a counter-cyclical manner, accumulating during a depression and declining in periods of prosperity. In view of this it can be generally assumed that raw materials at the beginning of a recovery period will be adequate to support an increased rate of manufacturing activity in the primary stages.[7] It cannot equally be assumed that this will be true throughout the intermediate and final manufacturing stages. For example, if inventories of cloth in the hands of the cloth manufacturer and the clothing manufacturer are at very low levels the latter might have to wait upon an increased production of cloth before he could begin to meet the increased orders he had received from the retailer. No general rule is applicable here and detailed knowledge of each industry would be required to form a true picture. The more rapid the rate of expansion, the more likely it would be that bottlenecks of this type would occur and this factor sets a limit on the rate of expansion which has no direct parallel during a period of recession. Since only finished goods at each stage of the manufacturing process will be available for shipment to supply the raw materials of the next stage of production, it is important to have a statistical breakdown at each stage showing inventories of raw materials, goods in process and finished goods, if adequate evidence on this point is to be obtained.

The point in question has been discussed by Keynes and Hawtrey. In his *Treatise on Money* Keynes argued that an expansion in economic activity would be slowed down by the lack of inventories at various stages of production. He argued further that an increased output of consumer goods would not become available until a full production period had elapsed from the time the increased production was undertaken.[8] In reply, Mr. Hawtrey pointed out that there was no reason why increased output could not begin at all stages of production at once provided some surplus stocks were available. Moreover, he argued, there is no reason why this increased output could not begin to add to stocks at all stages of production from the very beginning of a revival. In cases where shortages did occur, he pointed out, price increases would encourage a more rapid increase in output.[9] Hawtrey's position here is much sounder than Keynes'. Lack of inventories may place some restriction on the rate at which output can expand but it seems likely that this restrictive effect will be slight. Stocks of primary materials are usually excessive at the depth of the depression and the rise in the ratios of stocks to sales that occurs at all stages of production during a contraction would suggest that there are some surplus stocks at all stages of production. The evidence on this point will be examined in more detail in chapter XI.

The amount of goods actually in the process of production at any time is fixed within fairly narrow limits by technical considerations. Initially there is a small lead on the part of goods in process, and as the volume of production increases the amount of goods in process rises correspondingly. In addition, it will usually be convenient to carry a larger volume of raw materials and finished products at higher production levels. Because of this increase in inventories at all stages of production there tends to be a larger increase in the demand for primary commodities than for finally manufactured goods during an upswing in economic activity and a greater decline in demand during a downswing. Such fluctuations in the demand for primary commodities help to explain the counter-cyclical movement in stocks of primary commodities and the more extreme variation in the prices of raw materials over the business cycle.[10]

Special attention must also be given to an industry's relation to import or export trade. In a number of lines of manufacturing the raw materials used are primarily imported. This is particularly true in Canada of such industries as petroleum refining, sugar refining, cotton textiles, and rubber goods. In such instances, an increased investment in inventories will cause a proportionate increase in imports which will partially offset the stimulating influence of this increased investment. Increased payments made to firms or persons outside of Canada will not directly cause any increase in domestic employment or production. Similarly, during a period of falling activity, any disinvestment in inventories of imported goods will be reflected first in a decline in imports. Furthermore, because of the longer time required for delivery of imported goods it may take longer to adjust material stocks to the desired level in these industries. Though stocks of the imported commodity usually accumulate during a depression phase of the cycle, the importing country may not participate in this accumulation. Examination of individual circumstances is required here; some separate attention to industries dependent on an export market is also indicated. A decline in exports reflected in an initial accumulation of stocks may be the first indication of the impact of depressed activity in a foreign country. Here again, primary commodities, such as wheat, which tend to accumulate during a depression deserve separate attention.

We may conclude from the foregoing that it is necessary to classify inventories from several different points of view in order to assess properly the part they play in the business cycle. One important consideration is the relative rate and amount of change in the production and consumption of each commodity, because an accumulation or reduction in stocks is always the result of a difference between these two; it has thus been found desirable to classify commodities according to the degree to which they are subject to cyclical fluctuations in demand. This is partially, though not completely, related to the durability of the product. On the question of supply's special attention must be given to a group of commodities, primarily agricultural, for which production shows little cyclical fluctuation outside of that which may be imposed by cycles of climatic origin. But the conditions of supply for all commodities must receive consideration in order to determine whether their production can be readily adjusted to changes in demand. In tracing the flow of goods throughout the productive process some emphasis must be placed on the stage at which goods are held and whether they are in the form of raw materials or finished goods. Only finished goods are free to move on to the next stage of production and changes in demand will affect raw materials and finished goods differently. Finally the relation of each industry to the country's foreign trade requires attention.

CHAPTER SIX

THE RELATION OF PRICE CHANGES
TO CYCLICAL FLUCTUATIONS IN INVENTORIES

A USEFUL APPROACH for analysing the relation of price changes to fluctuations in inventories is to classify commodities on the basis of the timing, the degree, and the frequency of their price changes over the business cycle. It has been well established that prices of raw materials come first in all three respects. They lead, fluctuate more widely, and change more frequently over the cycle than prices of finished or semi-finished goods.[1] But this is not equally true of all raw materials: a distinction can be made between those whose prices are determined under conditions of keen competition, often on speculative, organized commodity exchanges, and those over which producers possess a substantial degree of monopoly. Prices of the latter, of which steel can be considered typical, are usually changed infrequently and fluctuate within rather narrow limits over the business cycle. It is not from these materials, but from the group of raw materials priced under competitive conditions, that raw material prices derive their cyclical pattern.

The greater degree of monopoly present seems to be a factor in the more rigid prices of semi-finished and finished commodities. Manufacturers frequently have some control over the market for their product and will set a price and then change it periodically in the light of market conditions. The more competitive the market, the more frequently they will be forced to change it, and the greater will be the degree of change over the cycle. Monopolies, on the other hand, frequently follow pricing policies which feature a high degree of stability.[2]

The cost of wages as well as the degree of monopoly affects the cyclical fluctuation of prices. Wage rates are among the more rigid costs in our economy, particularly during periods of depression when labour strongly resists wage reductions.[3] The greater degree of wage costs in finished goods helps to explain why they usually fluctuate less in price than raw materials. Other inflexible costs, such as excise taxes, transportation charges, and public utility rates, have a similar effect. Still other costs, such as interest, property taxes, and rents are also rigid, but these costs do not determine prices in the short run.

The degree to which prices change over the cycle is directly related to the elasticity of demand and supply and to the extent to which demand and supply shift during the cycle. In agriculture, where a large proportion of total costs including the labour of the farmer and his family are fixed, production falls off very little during periods of depression and increases rather slowly in periods of prosperity. This relatively inelastic supply in the face of a fluctuating and often inelastic demand causes extreme fluctuations in price. The same is true of some plantation products, such as coffee, rubber, and sugar. On the other hand, when a large proportion of total costs are variable from the enterpriser's standpoint, production falls off more sharply in the face of declining demand and the degree of price fluctuation is somewhat less extreme. This seems to be true of the prices of forest and mine products.

While no attempt has been made to document the preceding analysis in detail

TABLE 14

Wholesale Price Changes for Raw Materials and Finished Goods,

by Major Groups, Canada, 1929 to 1937

	Percentage decline 1929 high to 1932 low	Percentage increase 1933 low to 1937 high
Total Wholesale		
Raw and partly manufactured	50.1	74.5
Fully and chiefly manufactured	28.2	23.2
Farm Products, Field		
Raw and partly manufactured	65.8	159.3
Fully and chiefly manufactured	30.7	36.0
Farm Products, Animal		
Raw and partly manufactured	52.8	54.9
Fully and chiefly manufactured	42.4	34.3
Fishery Products		
Raw and partly manufactured	54.9	91.9
Fully and chiefly manufactured	44.3	21.4
Forest Products		
Raw and partly manufactured	35.5	15.3
Fully and chiefly manufactured	29.5	11.3
Mineral Products		
Raw and partly manufactured	19.7	19.8
Fully and chiefly manufactured	9.9	12.0

SOURCE: Canada, Dominion Bureau of Statistics, Annual Reports, 1929 to 1937, *Prices and Price Indexes.*

some supporting evidence is given in Tables 14 and 15. Table 14 shows the extremely sharp fluctuation that occurred in the price of agricultural products during the severe depression of the thirties. It also reveals the somewhat smaller fluctuations which occurred in the case of forest and mineral products. The degree of price change for fishery products was closely parallel to that of farm products, a reflection of the similar organization of the two industries. Both are characterized by a large number of independent enterprises and the extensive use of family labour. The greater fluctuation shown in the prices of raw materials and partly manufactured commodities is clearly evident in all types of products. Table 15 presents similar evidence for a number of commodity groups.

While the degree and frequency of change differ widely for different types of commodities, almost all price changes are closely related to the level of stocks or inventories. In discussing this relation, it is convenient to distinguish between primary raw materials, many of which are produced seasonally and semi-finished or fully manufactured goods. Variations in the level of stocks of the former are often accompanied by extreme fluctuations in price, owing to a number of factors.[4] Demand for these commodities—a derived demand—is often highly inelastic so that relatively small variations in total supply can cause extreme

TABLE 15

Wholesale Price Changes, Selected Commodities, Canada, 1929 to 1937

	Percentage decline 1929 high to 1932 low	Percentage increase 1933 low to 1937 high
Grains	72.5	321.3
Flour and other milled products	50.9	211.6
Bakery products	23.6	116.2
Hides and skins	81.5	436.5
Leather	40.7	143.5
Boots and shoes	20.6	108.2
Raw cotton	71.2	183.3
Yarn and thread	24.4	114.0
Cotton fabrics	17.2	105.7
Lumber and timber	38.2	162.3
Furniture	31.9	136.2
Pig Iron and steel billets	8.4	124.5
Hardware	6.0	105.9
Lead domestic	57.0	235.8
Lead pipe	2.5	189.5

SOURCE: Canada, Dominion Bureau of Statistics, Annual Reports, 1929 to 1937, *Prices and Price Indexes.*

variations in price. The additions to stocks of semi-finished goods and finished goods which occur during periods of prosperity and the depletion which occurs during periods of depression further accentuate fluctuations in the demand for primary materials. Moreover, the latter group includes many commodities whose production responds very slowly to changes in price. The output of agricultural commodities, in particular, is well maintained during periods of depression and this steady production in the face of a fluctuating demand contributes to extreme fluctuations in price. When these commodities can be stored, the degree of price fluctuation is partially explained by the fact that for these materials the annual carrying charges, including warehousing expenses, interest on invested capital, and insurance are high in relation to their value. This effect of carrying charges upon prices of primary commodities requires more extended consideration.[5]

Whenever surplus stocks appear, the current market price must fall far enough below normal (the price that would prevail in the absence of this surplus) to induce a contraction in output and an increase in consumption that will absorb this surplus. To explain price under these circumstances Mr. Keynes suggests the formula $x.y = p.q.$ in which x is the annual cost of carrying stocks measured as a per cent of normal price, y the surplus stocks as a per cent of a year's consumption, q the initial decline in output as a per cent of normal, and p the initial fall in price as a per cent of normal.[6] This formula implies that both price and output will immediately fall to a minimum and then gradually return to normal. It also assumes that there is an equal increase in consumption (q) and decline in production (also q) so that over the period as a whole the average rate at which stocks are absorbed will be equal to q. For example, consider a product such as wheat whose normal price is $1.00 per bushel, whose annual production and consumption is 100 million bushels and whose annual storage costs are 10¢ per bushel. Then suppose as a result of an unusually good crop a surplus of 20 million bushels develops. Thus x is 1/10 and y is 1/5. If in these circumstances a 20 per cent fall in prices is accompanied by a 10 per cent decrease in output (and a 10 per cent increase in consumption), the surplus will be absorbed in two years with prices gradually rising to normal in the meantime. On the other hand if output is very inelastic with relation to price the above equation might only be satisfied by a 50 per cent decline in price leading to a 4 per cent decline in output. Under such circumstances it would take five years to absorb the surplus stocks. It is clearly apparent that unless either supply or demand is quite elastic it may take a long time to absorb surplus stocks and in the interim prices may fall very low at first and only gradually return to normal.

In addition to other carrying charges which Keynes estimates would normally average about 10 per cent per annum, there is, he argues, an additional cost of carrying stocks in the form of the risk of changes in price.[7] The person or persons who assume the risk of holding stocks must be rewarded for incurring the risk of loss should prices decline.[8] This cost will be part of the total carrying costs (x) above and will tend to make necessary an even sharper decline in price to secure the absorption of surplus stocks. The amount of this additional cost may depend both on the existence of a body of professional speculators and the ease with which they can obtain credit to finance their operations.

One difficulty which must be faced in attempting to apply Mr. Keynes' theory is the fact, pointed out above, that in many cases stocks continue to accumulate until the depth of the depression and are only gradually absorbed as recovery sets in. Prices, of course, fall very sharply and Keynes' theory helps to explain why this occurs. But the final absorption of surplus stocks seems to be due mainly to the recovery in consumption which accompanies the upswing in the business cycle and only in small degree to the contraction of output or increase in consumption stimulated by the fall in prices. A question can be raised as to why prices do not fall still further if production does not decline below consumption sufficiently to cause some reduction in stocks. It would seem probable that there is an additional factor present, namely, the anticipation that prices will eventually rise. The prospect of gain from a rise in price must offset in part the risk of loss through a decline in prices. In some cases, of course, prices do fall to extremely low levels as they did in the thirties and if they continue at these levels will eventually force a sharp contraction in output. But, in the meantime, the prospect of recovery may keep prices from falling even further. This may also explain why prices continue to decline until surplus stocks reach their peaks and then move upwards rapidly as the surplus begins to be used up.

Crops that are produced at one season of the year show a seasonal fluctuation in both stocks and prices. The seasonal storage of these products distributes the annual output throughout the year to meet a steady year-round consumption. Here also prices will fluctuate throughout the year sufficiently to cover the cost of carrying supplies between crops.

Surplus stocks of non-storable raw materials or commodities that can be stored for a limited period of time will disappear fairly quickly. Under competitive conditions prices will fall sufficiently to force absorption of the surplus stocks within whatever period it is feasible to store them economically. Monopolies may prefer to adjust any surplus that develops by reducing output or even by destroying excessive stocks rather than by reducing prices.

There is also a close relation between prices and changes in stocks of manufactured goods not only at the manufacturing but throughout the wholesale and retail trade stages. Manufacturers usually exercise some degree of monopoly in the form of product differentiation or oligopoly. In such circumstances, while decisions on prices and output for the individual firm will be based on considerations of demand and cost, changes in stocks will often provide the indication that some adjustment in either prices or production is necessary. Following an initial increase in demand the manufacturer who is unable to meet it at once may allow his stocks of finished goods to decline. Eventually as stocks begin to reach minimum working levels he may consider raising his price. But even here many manufacturers seem to be reluctant to change their prices unless they consider it essential to meet a long-run change in demand and cost conditions. When it is the manufacturer's policy to keep his price fixed for relatively long periods, he may prefer to allow temporary shortages and informal rationing to develop rather than raise his prices during a period of urgent demand and he may often eliminate surplus stocks during a period of falling demand by cutbacks in production.[9] With more competition, manufacturers' prices usually advance more quickly in the face of declining stocks and are cut back sooner when stocks begin to mount. But even in this case, prices may not be changed to meet every temporary shortage. The numerous shortages of the recent post-war period provide ample testimony to this fact.

At the wholesale and retail levels a somewhat similar policy is followed. Here, however, it is customary to price goods by applying a fixed percentage markup to their laid down cost. These percentages are presumably based on what competition in the trade will allow and they provide a simple and convenient method of pricing. Markups may vary for different types of articles in the same store depending on such factors as handling costs, rate of turnover, and amount of spoilage. While adhering to these markups, stores will reduce prices by applying markdowns to slow-moving merchandise when stocks are accumulating. With seasonal goods such as clothing these markdowns usually take the form of end-of-season sales. Markdowns may also follow an unwise purchase or an unexpected shift in demand. Stores will be more likely to eliminate their surplus stocks of standard articles which are sold year in and year out, particularly those subject to resale price maintenance, by cutting down on their new purchases rather than by cutting prices. Similarly stores will increase their orders rather than advance prices when stocks are depleted. Retail dealers may sometimes take advantage of acute shortages by advancing prices to a level much beyond their usual markup. This occurred in Canada in fresh fruit and vegetable prices following the imposition of import restrictions in November, 1947.[10] But such instances seem to be exceptional. The dependence of these stores on their customers' goodwill makes it unwise to take full advantage of temporary shortages.

One Swedish writer G. Johansson has developed a theory based on the assumption that there are no surplus stocks at any stage of production.[11] It then follows that any increase in production must start at the raw material stage and gradually progress to the final stage of production. In the meantime the spending of incomes earned in the earlier stages will cause increased prices and profits in the final stages of output. As output gradually expands, prices and profits will decline in successive stages. This theory seems to conflict with the evidence that retail prices usually lag behind wholesale or manufacturers' prices while raw material prices tend to lead other prices over the cycle.[12] It seems more probable that there is some flexibility in the level of stocks carried at each stage and that the initial effect of an increase in consumer expenditures is a decline in retail inventories rather than an immediate advance in price.

However, it is true that at any stage of production shortages may sometimes be met by a temporary rise in prices which will serve as a stimulus for increased output to overcome the shortage. These shortages may often be bottlenecks

TABLE 16

Net Income of Farm Operators from Current Farm Production as a Percentage

of Net National Income, Canada, 1926 to 1947

1926	16.9	1937	8.1
1927	14.9	1938	9.3
1928	14.6	1939	10.7
1929	9.4	1940	9.7
1930	8.6	1941	8.3
1931	4.5	1942	13.0
1932	4.2	1943	11.7
1933	4.1	1944	12.5
1934	6.7	1945	9.9
1935	7.6	1946	11.6
1936	7.9	1947	11.2

Source: Canada, Dominion Bureau of Statistics, *National Accounts: Income and Expenditure, 1926-1947* (Ottawa, 1948).

which restrict a general advance in output. When the shortage is temporary it is most likely to be met by an increase in overtime work or the use of standby units rather than by a general expansion in plant capacity. Such bottlenecks are, of course, less likely to occur when there is widespread unemployment but may develop in some parts of the economy long before unemployment disappears. When the shortage is more permanent the higher prices serve to attract new resources into the field and tend to shift demand to substitute materials.

A major result of the sharp fluctuations in raw material prices that occur over the course of the cycle will be pronounced and rapid shifts in the distribution of income among different groups in our economy. Income of farmers and other producers of raw materials expands sharply during the upswing of a cycle and contracts drastically during a downswing. This is evident from the data given in Table 16; over the period 1926 to 1947 farm income in Canada varied from a high of 16.9 per cent of total income in 1926 to a low of 4.1 per cent in 1933. Similar shifts undoubtedly occurred in the proportion of income received by other producers of raw materials. Such shifts in income affect the stability of the marginal propensity to consume. There is some evidence that farmers on the average save a larger proportion of their income than other groups.[13] It would be reasonable to suppose that their marginal propensity to save might differ also. This will affect the shape of the savings schedule as the cyclical level of income changes. The effect of this on the equilibrium level of income will be discussed in more detail in chapter VII

The effect of price changes upon the income position of manufacturing, retail, and wholesale firms is highly dependent on the accounting method used in handling inventories. A recent study shows that most Canadian manufacturers use either average cost (46 per cent), first-in-first-out (15 per cent), or specific item cost (29 per cent); less than 5 per cent of the firms covered by the survey reported that they used a last-in-first-out method.[14] No study has yet been made of the methods used by retail and wholesale firms in Canada but it is generally known that the retail method, which gives a result somewhat similar to the first-in-first-out method is widely used. During a period of rising prices, reported profits will be much larger where an average cost, specific item cost, or a first-in-first-out method of inventory accounting is used, than they will under the last-in-first-out method. The reverse is true during a period of falling prices: reported profits will be much smaller or losses much larger under the former methods than they will where a last-in-first-out method is used. This arises out of the way in which materials are charged to sales.

Under the first-in-first-out method the firm will charge to its cost of goods sold the earliest purchases it has on hand. This means that during a period of rising prices the firm will continually be charging against its sales the cost of goods purchased several months earlier at lower prices. At the same time it will be replacing these goods in its inventory at the higher prices currently prevailing. Thus, while the firm will show an extra profit merely because it is charging to sales goods purchased at lower prices some time earlier, all of this extra profit will be required to finance its current purchases if its inventory is to be kept at the same level. Where the last-in-first-out method is used the firm will charge to sales its most recent purchases in point of time. In a period of rising prices these will be its highest priced purchases. For this reason its reported profits will be much lower than where a first-in-first-out method is used. At the same time, since it is charging its current high cost purchases to sales, the value of its inventory will not be increased by rising prices.

During a period of falling prices this situation is reversed. Under the first-in-first-out method a firm will now be charging to sales the materials it purchased several months earlier at higher prices. For this reason it will show a substantial loss or at the very least a much smaller profit. In contrast, with a last-in-first-out method, current purchases at the lower prices prevailing are charged to sales. Thus no loss is incurred because of the necessity of charging higher cost purchases to sales. These extra profits and losses which appear where a first-in-first-out method is used are often called inventory profits and inventory losses. The use of an average cost or specific item cost method gives a result fairly close to that obtained under the first-in-first-out method.

The situation is complicated during a period of falling prices by the widely used rule "lower of cost or market." Under this rule, at the end of its fiscal period a firm will write its inventory down to market price if this is lower than cost. This amount will be charged to sales thus further reducing reported profits and it is likely to be much larger where a first-in-first-out method is used than it is under a last-in-first-out method, particularly if the latter method was first introduced in a period of low prices. In actual fact, this rule is not usually used in conjunction with a last-in-first-out method although there seems to be no theoretical objection to its use in this instance.

Thus it can be seen that the most widely used methods of inventory accounting accentuate reported business profit and loss over the business cycle.[15] While business men may be partially aware of the existence of these inventory losses, particularly in periods of rapidly changing prices, it is doubtful if they discount them completely.[16] The inventory profits earned during the upswing of a cycle will help to increase business optimism, this in turn will increase capital spending and dividend payments and reinforce the upswing. Similarly during the downswing inventory losses will reinforce business pessimism and accelerate the downswing.

If business firms base increased dividend payments or capital expenditures on their higher reported profits even when these are entirely inventory profits, they will find it necessary to finance at least part of their increased inventory values out of borrowed funds. This increase in spending will have a net expansionary or inflationary effect on the economy. In a period of declining prices the reverse will be true. Part of the proceeds from the decline in inventory values may be used to retire bank loans or pay off other debts. This will have a contractionary or deflationary influence,[17] partially offset by the fact that firms whose reported profits are inflated by inventory profits will be forced to pay larger amounts out in taxes thus decreasing their cash position as compared with firms using last-in-first-out or similar methods. However, the consequent reduction in capital spending may be offset by the easier access to capital markets of firms with larger reported profits.[18]

In addition to the inventory accounting method used, the basis on which the selling price is determined may affect the profits obtained by the firm. It has been tacitly assumed above that selling prices were based on current replacement costs. However, in the survey of Canadian manufacturing firms referred to above only about 45 per cent gave replacement cost as the most important factor in determining selling price. For the remainder it was actual cost, which would reflect their particular method of inventory accounting. While economists have given relatively little attention to this point in dynamic theory they apparently incline to the view that prices should be based on current replacement costs. This view seems to be the basis for the inventory revaluation adjustment which is included in estimates of national income.[19]

When selling price is based on actual rather than replacement cost a firm's reported profits will not be inflated during a period of rising prices even though it uses a first-in-first-out or average cost method of accounting. This same firm may find itself forced to obtain additional credit, perhaps by bank loans, to finance the increased value of its normal working inventory. Similarly, during a period of falling prices the firm may incur no inventory losses and may find that it can repay its bank loans as the value of its inventory declines. The additional funds placed in circulation during the upswing and withdrawn during the downswing of the cycle will tend to reinforce cyclical swings. Though it is difficult to assess the over-all importance of this type of phenomenon it is clear that it exists in certain instances. At the manufacturing stage it is prevalent among firms that produce goods to binding orders, particularly the heavy capital goods industries such as railway rolling stock, shipbuilding, aircraft, machinery, and heavy electrical equipment. The accounting method most frequently used by these firms is specific item cost.[20] They can buy their materials against a specific order and calculate a normal amount of profit on the basis of actual manufacturing cost using these materials; meanwhile, they may be replacing these materials at higher prices against additional orders. They are thus protected against subsequent prices changes. There is also some evidence that prices are based on actual manufacturing cost in industries which possess a substantial degree of monopoly such as the tobacco, distilling, and brewing industries. Here the emphasis, in any case, is on price stability and the industry apparently has sufficient control over its selling price that it can still maintain a profit during a period of declining raw material prices even though its inventory is on an average cost basis. In retail channels there is also evidence that the retailer may price his goods by applying a markup to actual cost while at the same time replacing them with higher priced merchandise.[21] Here again there is a rise in inventory values but no inventory profit with which to finance them. This is likely to be true especially of stores with marked seasonal patterns in their sales.

The lack of complete adherence to a replacement cost basis of pricing undoubtedly helps to explain why prices of raw materials or goods at an early stage in the productive process tend to lead prices of finished commodities over the cycle. Complete adherence to pricing on a replacement cost basis would result in closer correspondence in the timing of price changes at various stages of the economy.

With present methods of inventory accounting, then, the rise and fall in prices will cause an increase and decrease in the money value of a given volume of inventories, which in turn will exert an effect on the economy in addition to any change in the physical volume of inventories. The extent of this effect will vary, depending on whether selling prices are based on current replacement cost or on actual cost.

If all prices are based on current replacement cost, any change in prices will cause an almost proportional change in the value of inventories and a substantial change in profits. As was argued above, this rise and fall in the value of inventories is likely to have an expansionary and contractionary effect. These effects would be minimized if the windfall nature of these profits and losses were recognized so that they had little effect on business optimism, dividend payments, or capital spending. The fact that part of these inventory profits must be paid to the government in tax tends to minimize any expansionary effect. Nevertheless, it seems probable that on balance the rise and fall in the value of inventories resulting from price changes will exert a substantial expansionary and contractionary effect on the economy in all industries where prices are based on current replacement cost.

When account is taken of those industries in which selling prices are based on actual rather than replacement cost this conclusion is reinforced. In such industries the rise and fall in the value of a given volume of inventories as a result of price changes will not cause any corresponding windfall profits. Nevertheless all of the increase or decrease in the value of inventories will be reflected in increased or decreased incomes elsewhere in the economy. The increased value of inventories will create a corresponding demand for funds to finance it; similarly the decreased value of inventories which results from a price fall is likely to take funds out of the spending stream. If business firms that operate on this basis resort to bank loans to finance the rise in the value of their inventory they will probably repay these loans when the value of their inventory falls.

Thus, for the Canadian economy as a whole, the rise and fall in the value of inventories resulting from price changes will exert an important expansionary and contractionary effect on the economy. When prices are based on current replacement costs the rise and fall in the value of inventory will cause corresponding inventory profits and losses which may cause increased capital spending and dividend payments. The payment of taxes out of this income and its utilization in part to finance the increased value of inventories will partially offset the expansionary effect. When prices are based on actual accounting costs, corresponding offsetting effects are likely to arise only if the firm is forced to curtail its dividend payments or other capital expenditures in order to finance the increase in the value of its inventory.

The effect of these considerations on the conclusions reached in earlier chapters is somewhat difficult to assess. I had previously concluded that when no lags in expenditure were present inventories would remain at a stationary level only when income was at an equilibrium level; only at this income level would the production of goods exactly match consumers' expenditures. But if prices rise when goods are in short supply or fall when there is a surplus of particular commodities, the difference between consumers' expenditures and production will be reflected partially in changes in prices and not entirely through changes in inventories. These price changes also alter the distribution of income and thus affect the savings schedule and the equilibrium level of income. This is particularly true of the prices of raw materials and farm products. In general it appears that the effect of price changes would be the modification of unwanted changes in inventories. If unexpected increases in expenditures are causing a decline in retailers' stocks this will be partially checked by advancing prices. Similarly if retailers find themselves overstocked they may at least partially liquidate these stocks by sharp reductions in price. Further, the rise and fall in the value of a given volume of inventories which accompanies a rise and fall in prices exerts an additional expansionary and contractionary effect on the economy. An increase in the value of total inventories as a result of a rise in prices exerts an effect similar to that of an increase in other forms of investment; it raises the equilibrium level of income as defined above, and thus makes it more difficult for business firms to achieve a planned addition to the volume of their inventories. The opposite is true in a period of falling prices. The decline in the value of inventories has an effect similar to that of a net reduction in other forms of investment; it reduces the equilibrium level of income and makes it more difficult for business firms to achieve a planned reduction in the volume of their inventories. But the effects of a rise or fall in the value of inventories as a result of price changes are likely to be smaller than those of a similar change in other forms of investment. The effects of changes in the value of inventories are lessened by the lower rate of spending out of inventory profits, by the tax drain out of these profits and by restrictions which may arise in the firm's access to funds from the banking system or through the capital market.

CHAPTER SEVEN

EXPENDITURE ON CONSUMERS' SERVICES AND INVENTORY FLUCTUATIONS

THUS FAR it has been assumed that inventories were valued at retail prices. This has enabled a direct comparison of the production of consumer goods with consumers' expenditures and has made possible the assumption that an increase in consumers' spending would result in an equal decline in the value of inventories. This would be approximately true if the retailer's markup were negligible, but this is not the case; the average markup by Canadian retail stores in 1941 was about 20 per cent.[1] In effect it has been assumed that retailers count their profits on any increase in their stocks at the time these changes occur instead of when the goods are finally sold. This has meant that certain items have been treated as income and hence available for expenditure before they actually became income. It is now important to examine how the retailer's markup affects the results obtained in the earlier models.

It has also been assumed that all consumers' expenditures were made on goods sold out of inventory, whereas a substantial proportion of these expenditures are for services which have little relation to inventories. Since income earned by the retailer in selling goods to the public is essentially similar to other forms of consumers' services the implications of both of these assumptions can be examined at once.

In Canada the expenditure of consumers on services has remained a fairly stable percentage of their total expenditures. This percentage increased from about 36 per cent in the period 1926 to 1929 to 39 per cent in 1932 and then declined to 34.5 per cent in 1940. Since the introduction of rent control the proportion of total expenditures devoted to services has declined. It averaged only 29.4 per cent for the period 1941 to 1950. More variability has been shown by the year-to-year increase or decrease in expenditure on services calculated as a percentage of the corresponding change in total consumers' expenditures. This ratio has varied from as high as 74 per cent to as low as 10 per cent and in two years the totals moved in opposite directions. Most of this variability is due to the lag in rents behind other prices. Over the period 1926 to 1950 the average year-to-year change in expenditure on services as a percentage of the corresponding change in total spending was about 30 per cent. If to this were added one-fifth of the year-to-year changes in expenditures on goods a total of 44 per cent would be obtained. This would suggest that on the average some 44 per cent of all changes in expenditures are for services, where services are defined to include the retailers' markup on goods, but that there may be marked variations from this percentage in particular years.

Expenditures on services differ from expenditures on goods in a number of respects. An increase in expenditures for services results in no equivalent decline in inventories. Instead there is an immediate increase in output and income. For this reason increased expenditures on services lead to an increase in income which is available at once for further expenditure. If all expenditures were for services the lag between output and sales would be zero. Further, for a period of one month increased expenditures on services lead to increased income in the service industry which may be re-expended within the same month. This will depend on how quickly income is paid out and on who receives it. Some light is thrown on this problem by Table 17 which shows the relative importance in one year of the main types of service expenditure in Canada.

TABLE 17

Consumers' Expenditures on Services, Canada, 1941

	$ million	Per cent
Shelter (rent etc.)	710	43.5
Personal Care, medical care and death expenses	277	17.0
User operated and purchased transportation	184	11.3
Telephone, gas, and electricity	114	7.0
Motion picture theatres	41	2.5
Laundering and dry cleaning	36	2.2
Miscellaneous	269	16.5
Total	1,631	100.0

SOURCE: Canada. Dominion Bureau of Statistics, *National Accounts: Income and Expenditure 1926-1950* (Ottawa, 1952) and *National Accounts: Income and Expenditure 1941-1948* (Ottawa, 1949).

The most important type of service expenditure is residential rent. In 1941 rent and lodging including imputed rents of home owners amounted to 43.5 per cent of total service expenditures. During a recovery period the reduction in vacancies and the gradual rise in the level of rents would probably account for the major part of the increased expenditure on rents. As vacancies disappeared construction of new houses for rental purposes would also become important. In each case the increased rent paid would go to swell the net rents of landlords. If landlords, in the main, are a class with an above-average income the propensity to spend out of this type of income would be below average. For other types of service expenditure it is difficult to reach any conclusions without a more detailed study. If agriculture is excepted, unincorporated enterprise is more important in the service industries than elsewhere. Roughly two-thirds of all income earned by non-farm, unincorporated enterprises is earned in the service industries. But when account is taken of the agricultural sector unincorporated enterprise is of about equal relative importance in the production of goods and of services. In addition to the conclusions reached about the income of landlords, the fact that almost all professional income is included in the service sector would suggest that on the average the propensity to spend out of income earned in the service industry might be below average. However, not much confidence can be placed in this conclusion.

The service industry also differs from the production of goods in another respect. Increased output of goods may occur either because sales have increased or because the individual producer decides independently of current sales to increase his output. He might decide to do this either because he wishes to add to his inventory or because he expects an increase in sales in the near future. But in the service industry activity depends entirely on expenditures. The industry cannot increase its output except in response to increased expenditures on the part of its customers. A barber, for example, can only work when he has customers. Sales might be stimulated by advertising or changes in price but the scope for causing a general increase in sales and hence in output by this method is likely to be extremely limited. And of course the same methods of increasing sales are also available to the manufacturer. The latter, in addition, is free to increase production without awaiting an increase in sales, assuming, of course, that funds are available to finance this increased expenditure.

On the average, then, about 40 to 50 per cent of any increase or decrease in expenditure will be for services. In contrast to that for goods, any increase in expenditures for services is immediately available for re-expenditure; the lag between output and sales is zero. On the other hand, since the output of services cannot be increased independently of the level of consumers' expenditure, services cannot be produced for inventory. The initiative concerning any change in the level of output comes almost entirely from the expenditure side.

What effect does allowance for the service content of expenditure have on our previous models? Since 40 to 50 per cent of any change in consumers' expenditures is for services, fluctuations in inventories will be reduced proportionately. In Table 1 the initial decline in inventories would be substantially smaller. The relative importance of inventories as a cause or effect of cyclical fluctuations is smaller than our previous models have suggested. The inclusion of services should also affect any assumptions made as to lags in expenditure. In Model 2 it was assumed that an increase or decrease in income would cause a change in expenditure, partially within the period in which the income was earned, partially with a lag of one period. In general the presence of services should make lags in expenditure somewhat shorter for an initial increase in expenditure for services may create increased income which will be respent within the same month. Moreover, it was argued in chapter IV that lags in expenditures tend to reduce the magnitude of unplanned fluctuations in inventories. Accordingly, to the extent that services reduce the importance of these lags they will increase the importance and magnitude of unplanned fluctuations in inventories. Thus, the two principal results of the introduction of services affect the models in opposite directions. On the whole, it seems probable that the former effect will be the stronger and that the importance of involuntary fluctuations in inventories is reduced when account is taken of services.

CHAPTER EIGHT

INVESTMENT EXPENDITURES, THE GOVERNMENT. THE SAVINGS SCHEDULE, AND INVENTORY FLUCTUATIONS

THUS FAR it has been assumed that investment in durable assets is made independently of the level of income and consumption, an assumption which requires further examination. In the current literature capital spending is often considered to be a function of one or more of the following: the rate of interest, the rate of change in consumers' expenditures, the level of income, and the level of expected profits. While it is beyond the scope of this work to examine in any detail all the factors which determine the level of capital investment in our society, a brief survey of the more important determinants of investment will help to complete our model of the economic system.

In an enterprise society net investment is closely connected with growth or change. Zero net investment, the mere replacement of existing plant and equipment as it wears out, would enable continued production of the present level of goods and services.[1] If population is growing some net investment will be required to maintain a constant per capita output of goods and services. Some of this net investment may take the form of the development of new resources or the settlement of new land areas or frontiers. In addition, if the per capita level of consumption is growing or is to grow, net investment will be necessary to enable this to take place and will be stimulated by these rising standards of consumption. The effect of new techniques or new products on net investment is less certain. In part, new inventions such as television may stimulate an increased level of per capita consumption and increased investment. But new inventions may also cause a diversion of expenditures away from other fields; television may divert expenditures away from radio and motion pictures. Where there is such a diversion of expenditures an increase in net investment may or may not occur; the outcome will depend on whether the increased investment required for the development of the new product exceeds the disinvestment caused in the older industries.[2] For maintaining the existing level of output even a regular flow of new techniques requiring the introduction of new improved machinery would not result in net investment if the concept of depreciation covers some normal (however defined) rate of obsolescence. Here again, the outcome is uncertain: the new techniques may involve the use of more capital than those which they replace; they might equally well be capital-saving. But where the new techniques lead to a rise in per capita output they make possible an increase in per capita consumption and this may be an important source of new investment. Since investment is undertaken in the expectation of making a profit, a reduction in the cost of investment either because of a lower rate of interest or lower prices for investment goods would stimulate increased investment. But while a reduction in investment costs will bring additional projects within the range of profitable investment these projects serve the same fundamental purposes; they raise the level of per capita consumption or make an increased amount of leisure time available.

In the short run, additional considerations are important. Individual investments are, to use Robertson's term, "lumpy." They take time to get started and time to finish. In many cases it is impracticable to leave them in a partially completed state. The durability of investments is also important. A lower rate of interest might encourage the construction of more durable capital assets, for example more durable houses, which would temporarily involve a higher level of investment.

The relation between consumption and investment is known as the acceleration principle. In essence this principle is equivalent to the point made above, namely, that net investment is fundamentally related to increased consumption whether the latter is due to population growth or a rise in per capita consumption. In discussing this relation emphasis is usually placed on the causal influence of the rate of change in consumption or output upon the rate of investment. For the increased production of existing goods and services connected with population growth, this emphasis is undoubtedly correct. But for increased consumption of new products the initiative may often be largely on the side of the investor. The development of new products involving an initial investment may stimulate demand and lead to higher consumption. Moreover even in the former instance it is a mistake to insist on too rigid a connection between consumption and investment. This is particularly true in the short run. The existence of excess capacity, which is widespread in periods of substantial unemployment, the use of standby units, and the ability to work overtime or extra shifts introduce a good deal of flexibility in the relation that exists between the volume of consumption and the stock of capital equipment. Further, increased demand for particular types of capital equipment or for capital equipment in general is sharply limited, once full employment is approached, by the capacity of the investment goods industry. Shortages of skilled labour, the time required to train new workers, and shortages of basic materials like steel and cement, which in turn appear to be limited by a monopoly organization of industry and a fear of over-development, all limit the extent to which investment can increase in the short run. The widespread accumulation of backlogs of orders in the machinery and basic materials industries provides a further indication that increased output of capital goods is limited.[3] Finally higher prices for early delivery can serve to ration capital goods though the importance of grey markets in the post-war period would suggest that many suppliers prefer a more informal method of rationing.[4] All these arguments support the belief that the acceleration principle has more validity as a long-run description of the relation between consumption and investment than as a mechanism for explaining the course of the business cycle.[5]

In using the acceleration principle to explain the course of the business cycle it is quite common to argue in the following way. Suppose an upward movement in activity commences in a period of depression. The rise in income leads to an increase in consumption and once excess capacity begins to disappear this will lead to an increase in investment. The level of investment will be geared to the rate at which consumption is increasing. But since consumption must level off once full employment is approached the decline in the rate of increase in consumption will lead to an absolute fall in net investment and, indeed, in gross investment, according to most observers.[6] This argument neglects an important consideration. If, at the peak of the preceding boom, the volume of capital equipment was adequate to support a full employment level of consumption, and if, as seems true of most cycles, no actual reduction in the quantity of capital takes place during the ensuing depression, why should the acceleration principle operate at all before the system has returned to a point of full employment? There is, of course, some continued population growth and there may be a decline in the marriage and birth rates during periods of contraction so that population may begin to grow more rapidly when income begins to rise again. This would create an increased demand for investment. In addition, replacements may be deferred during the contraction in the face of falling prices, excess capacity, and restricted credit so that there is an abnormal increase in replacements during a period of expansion. These factors explain why the secular growth in the demand for capital may be interrupted during periods of depression and backlogs of demand or potential demand for capital goods may develop. The existence of these backlogs will give a special impetus to the demand for capital goods during a recovery period. But this does not imply that the demand for capital goods will be insufficient once the backlog has disappeared. In the long-range view it is not true that consumption must cease to grow once full employment is reached. It is the secular rise in consumption that is the primary cause and effect of capital investment.

There is good reason to believe that investment is, to an important extent, a function of income. By this I mean that, with a given level of expected profit, business firms and individuals are more likely to make an investment expenditure when they can finance part of it out of their current income. This is a question both of willingness and of ability to invest. When a person is investing his own funds the risk of non-repayment is absent; the risk incurred is that of losing a part or all of his present capital. Such a risk may be viewed as substantially less than the risk of going, into debt through the loss of borrowed funds. Reinvestment of current earnings is much simpler for a corporation than raising capital through a new issue of shares or a bond issue. The issue of shares usually requires special approval at a meeting of the stockholders, who often dislike such a dilution of their equity. A bond issue increases the firm's fixed payments and hence the danger that in time of depression the firm may be unable to meet its obligations, a contingency which, if realized, might easily result in the present owners' losing control of the firm.[7] In addition, a business firm may often reinvest its own earnings even though it does not expect as high a rate of return as could be obtained on the current capital market. Such reinvestment is particularly likely to occur in large corporations controlled by management or minority stockholder interests. Management tends to identify itself with its own company and likes to see the company grow and expand. Moreover, as Keynes has suggested, reinvestment "will protect the management from criticism, since increasing income due to accumulation is seldom distinguished from increasing income due to efficiency."[8]

Increased income also increases an individual's or business firm's *ability* to invest. Anyone who has recently purchased a house will be well aware that the ability to invest in a house is substantially dependent on the ability to make a cash down payment. This down payment is much easier to make when a person is in a position to save something out of his current income. Experience with instalment finance of durable goods has demonstrated that the consumer's ability and willingness to buy is often more dependent on the size of the initial down payment required and the length of time over which the balance must be repaid than on the amount of the interest charge. It seems probable that this is also true of the purchase of most capital goods. The firm or individual in a position to finance a substantial down payment out of current income will find it much easier to obtain funds to finance the balance. Thus, while in the long run investment is closely related to underlying growth factors in the economy, in the short run it is heavily dependent on the current level of income.[9] If business firms' expectations are also related to the level of income and the current level of profits, this argument is reinforced.

Thus, to explain the cyclical variation in investment, investment will be treated partly as a function of income and partly as a function of the stage in the business cycle. While the exact relation between investment and income is uncertain an attempt will be made to set forth a plausible representation of it. It seems clear that in the trough of a depression when there is an abundance of idle equipment and resources an increase in income will have less effect on investment than it would at higher levels of activity when most equipment is in use. Nevertheless, some positive relation would be expected. As the economy moves to higher levels of income and existing equipment is more fully utilized each increase in income will lead to a larger increase in investment. But once the capital goods industry approaches capacity in its operations, a stage which may well coincide with full employment in society generally, the investment function is likely to level off. With any further increase in income, investment will face sharply rising costs and business firms may find increasing difficulty in obtaining credit to finance investment.

In addition, it has been argued here that the level of investment will depend on the stage of the cycle in which the economy happens to be. Thus at the beginning of a recovery period some business firms may wish to increase their capacity when costs are favourable, so they will be prepared to meet increased demands of a later date. If replacements have been deferred during the preceding contraction, this delayed demand will reinforce the demand for investment goods during the expansion. Mr. R. S. Sayers has suggested that technical improvements seem to be adopted more readily once recovery is well underway but before prosperity has become widespread.[10] The rising marriage and birth rate will also increase the demand for capital goods in a period of growing prosperity. Planned additions to stocks and the rise in the value of inventories caused by higher prices will add to other forms of investment. A rising level of income may cause an increase in business optimism which will in turn lead to further investment and a further rise in income. Inventory profits which accompany a period of rising income will also increase business optimism and cause a further rise in investment.[11] All of these factors would tend to make investment larger during a period of expansion than it would be if investment were a function of income alone. Conversely during a contraction in economic activity these factors would operate in the opposite direction; they would tend to make investment lower than it would be on the basis of income alone.

A graphic representation of such an investment function is given in Chart 2. In this chart money income is measured on the x axis and money investment on the y axis. The investment function II shows the volume of gross investment which would occur at each level of income (defined as gross national product). This graph shows that if any particular level of income were to persist it would tend to call forth the corresponding amount of gross investment shown by the investment function II. In addition the dotted lines above and below this function show the level of investment that would occur when the stage of the business cycle is taken into consideration. During the expansion, investment

CHART 2

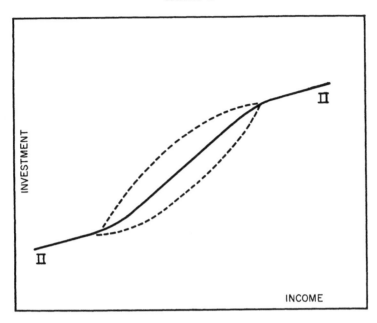

The Investment Function

would tend to follow the upper dotted line, during the contraction it would tend to follow the lower. These two dotted lines involve more dynamic considerations since they are due to factors which call forth temporary additions to or subtractions from the level of investment that would occur on the basis of income alone.[12] General changes in optimism or pessimism would cause the whole curve to shift upwards or downwards.

The use of money (in terms of current dollars) as opposed to real magnitudes for investment, saving, and income calls for a word of explanation. It is assumed that prices will rise and fall by some (undefined) normal amount during a cyclical expansion and contraction. The decision to invest and the decision to save are no doubt based to a considerable extent on real considerations and this would suggest the use of real magnitudes. But the equilibrium level of income can be accurately defined only in terms of current dollar magnitudes. If during some periods prices of capital goods rise more than the prices of goods in general, the desired volume of real investment will only be realized at an income level where the community is willing to save an amount equal to the money value of this investment. This might involve a larger amount of real savings than would occur if investment goods prices were lower Decisions to save and to invest will be reflected in monetary magnitudes even though partially based on real magnitudes.[13]

Having reached these tentative conclusions regarding the investment function it is next necessary to examine more closely our initial assumptions about the stability and shape of the savings or consumption function. These two functions taken together make it possible to determine the equilibrium level of income— our reference point for the analysis of an accumulation or liquidation of inventories. However, before considering the various factors that determine the shape of the savings function it is useful to make a few assumptions about government revenues and expenditures. It is assumed that the government adopts a policy of keeping its tax rates constant and budgets for a small surplus at a full employment level of income. When activity declines the government budget is automatically pushed into a deficit position as a result of a decline in revenues with constant tax rates and an increase in transfer expenditures for the support of any unemployed who have exhausted their insurance benefits. It is assumed that in real terms other types of government expenditures remain constant. For purposes of our analysis of savings and investment a government deficit is treated as negative saving, a government surplus as positive saving.

To reach some conclusions about the shape and stability of the savings function it is also necessary to form some idea of the relative importance of different components of the gross savings function. Table 18 shows the main components of gross private savings in Canada for the period 1926 to 1955 (the war years 1942-45 excepted). Depreciation allowances and similar business costs are the most important components but because of their relative stability in absolute magnitude they show a tendency to decline in importance in years of prosperity and increase in periods of depression. A substantial part of such depreciation

TABLE 18

Composition of Gross Private Savings, Canada, 1926 to 1955

| | Per cent of Gross Savings | | | | | |
	1926-29	1930-33	1934-37	1938-41	1946-50	1951-55
Personal saving	26.7	— 7.8	8.4	28.4	30.9	30.1
Undistributed corporate profits	18.8	—19.4	16.6	16.3	22.9	16.4
Depreciation etc.	54.5	127.2	75.0	55.3	46.2	53.5
Personal savings and depreciation	52.5	51.7	43.0	50.7	49.8	50.5
Corporate saving and depreciation	47.5	48.3	51.0	49.3	50.2	49.5

SOURCE: Canada, Dominion Bureau of Statistics, *National Accounts: Income and Expenditure, 1926-1950* (Ottawa, 1952), and *ibid., 1950-1955* (Ottawa, 1956).

allowances, including almost all of those on farm property and residental real estate, are in the hands of unincorporated businesses or individuals. Individuals or businesses of this type may keep no record of depreciation and may simply treat these receipts as part of their current income. Even for corporations the dividing line between income and an allowance for capital consumption is often arbitrary. Both net income and depreciation allowances are a source of cash that the corporation may use either for making capital expenditures or for paying dividends or bond interest. For this reason Table 18 shows the relative importance of personal savings plus depreciation allowances of individuals and unincorporated business, and corporate savings plus depreciation allowances of corporations.

Taken by themselves, both personal savings and undistributed corporate profits became negative in the early 1930's. But the totals for each, including depreciation, remained positive in all years. With the disappearance of inventory losses in 1933 corporate profits showed a substantial recovery and in the period 1934 to 1937 undistributed corporate profits were a larger proportion of gross private savings than were personal savings. The most important change in the savings pattern between the years 1926 to 1929 and the recent period 1946 to 1950 has been the relative decline in depreciation allowances. This undoubtedly reflects the inadequacy of allowances based on original cost during a period of rising prices. Most of this decline is centred in the non-corporate sector. Within the past five years, however, depreciation allowances have recovered most of their former importance.

According to the evidence presented in Table 9, corporate profits tend to increase rapidly during periods of expansion and fall off rapidly during periods of contraction. However, there is evidence that although corporate profits increase rapidly during an expansion from low levels of income, once a high level of employment is reached the share of any further increase in income received in the form of corporate profits is reduced. Thus between 1946 and 1950 the increase in corporate profits before tax was only 14.1 per cent of the increase in gross national product. Since a large proportion of corporate profits are saved, either in the form of undistributed profits or in the form of personal savings out of dividend payments, these changes in corporate profits will tend to create a similar pattern in the gross savings function. The influence of changes in the relative share of corporate profits in total income will tend to make the marginal propensity to save out of gross national product comparatively large whenever income is below a level of full employment; it will tend to make the marginal propensity to save somewhat smaller at full employment income levels [14]

Data for savings out of personal disposable income reveal a similar pattern. Table 19 presents evidence that personal savings as a percentage of disposable income fluctuate over a moderate range during years of high employment but fall off sharply in years of depression. Thus in the period 1926 to 1929 this percentage varied within the range of 6.4 and 8.7 per cent. More variation in the proportion of income saved occurred during the period 1946 to 1955 but

TABLE 19

Personal Savings as a Percentage of Personal Disposable Income,
Canada, 1926 to 1955*

1926	8.7	1934	0.6	1942	16.8	1950	4.1
1927	6.4	1935	1.5	1943	24.7	1951	7.2
1928	8.4	1936	2.3	1944	25.2	1952	8.2
1929	6.9	1937	4.2	1945	21.4	1953	9.2
1930	1.0	1938	3.3	1946	11.6	1954	6.4
1931	.3	1939	5.9	1947	5.2	1955	6.1
1932	—4.0	1940	7.1	1948	9.6		
1933	—2.8	1941	10.5	1949	8.9		

* Personal savings and personal income are both adjusted to exclude net changes in farm inventories.
SOURCE: *National Accounts: Income and Expenditure, 1926-1950*, and *ibid., 1950-1955*.

this is not surprising in view of the backlog of demand for durable assets that existed at the end of the war and the large volume of liquid assets held by consumers. During the early thirties personal savings fell off very sharply and were negative in 1932 and 1933. Thus the data for personal savings also supports the conclusion reached with respect to corporate profits that the marginal propensity to save will be comparatively large during periods when the economy is operating below capacity but will decline once income approaches capacity.

This general pattern is reflected in Table 20 which presents data on total gross private savings as a percentage of gross private disposable income (gross national product plus government transfer payments less all taxes). These data indicate that the proportion of gross private disposable income saved in years of high employment has remained remarkably stable. Thus with the exception of the two years 1929 and 1947 this proportion varied within the narrow range

TABLE 20

Gross Private Savings as a Percentage of Gross Private Disposable Income,
Canada, 1926 to 1955

1926	21.8	1934	15.9	1942	34.2	1950	21.0
1927	22.1	1935	17.1	1943	34.5	1951	23.0
1928	22.7	1936	16.4	1944	34.8	1952	22.7
1929	19.8	1937	19.9	1945	30.7	1953	23.8
1930	15.9	1938	18.3	1946	22.7	1954	21.2
1931	11.8	1939	22.2	1947	19.7	1955	23.2
1932	8.6	1940	23.8	1948	22.6		
1933	9.8	1941	25.3	1949	21.1		

SOURCE: *National Accounts: Income and Expenditure, 1926-1950*, and *ibid., 1950-1955.*

of 21.0 to 23.8 per cent during the fourteen high employment years 1926 to 1929 and 1946 to 1955. The year 1929 also falls within this range if an adjustment is made for the liquidation in farm inventories that occurred in that year. The proportion of gross private disposable income saved declined sharply during the 1930's.

On the basis of this analysis it seems reasonable to conclude that the gross savings function will rise fairly rapidly when income is below capacity but will tend to flatten out so that a more or less constant proportion of income is saved once a full employment level is reached. Though no use is made of precise estimates of the savings function in this study it is useful to note that in Canada the marginal propensity to save, defined as the change in gross private saving expressed as a percentage of the corresponding change in gross private disposable income, was about 34 per cent from 1929 to 1933, about 41 per cent from 1933 to 1937, about 17 per cent from 1946 to 1950, and about 24 per cent from 1951 to 1955.

These conclusions are based on statistical estimates of savings which, in addition to being subject to statistical errors, may differ from planned or intended savings because of the inclusion of unintended components of savings resulting from unexpected increases or decreases in income. These savings estimates may also include the effects of lags in expenditure. Moreover, it is quite possible that the underlying savings function may have shifted during this period. Despite these qualifications I believe that the underlying savings pattern described above is valid. Although the personal savings function may sometimes shift substantially, personal savings are only one part of the total savings function and the total savings function appears to show a considerable measure of stability.

Up to this point it has been assumed that any increase or decrease in investment expenditures on plant and equipment causes an immediate increase or decrease in the output of investment goods. This need not be so. An increase in investment expenditures for building and equipping a new factory may result in some reduction in inventories of building materials and machinery. Furthermore, changes in the production of investment materials may occur independently of changes in actual investment expenditures for plant and equipment. Inventories of these materials can be accumulated in anticipation of improved demand or reduced when a downturn is expected. However, it seems likely that the direct effect of investment expenditures on inventories will not be large. Many capital goods are made to order—this applies both to machinery and equipment and to the construction of factories and other buildings—here, the possible decline in inventories as a result of an increased demand for investment goods will be limited to the inventories of materials carried by firms producing machinery and equipment and the inventories of contractors in the construction industry or to inventories carried by suppliers of these two groups.

When this particular assumption is dropped the conclusions reached in the first model in chapter III are not fundamentally affected. It will still be true that inventories can only accumulate when income exceeds the equilibrium level and will decline as long as income remains below the equilibrium level. One difference will be that part of this reduction or accumulation of inventories will be in the investment goods industry. A further difference is that the equilibrium level of income will only be reached when the production of both investment and consumer goods are at their appropriate levels. These levels are achieved when the production of investment goods has increased to the level of investment expenditures on durable assets and the production of consumer goods has increased to the equilibrium level of consumer expenditures—the amount that would be made at the equilibrium level of income. A less restrictive condition of equilibrium would obtain when the combined production of investment goods and consumer goods yielded an equilibrium level of income.[15]

The more detailed analysis of the saving and investment function that was made above permits some reassessment of the conclusions reached in the earlier chapters.[16] In chapter III it was argued that an accumulation of inventories would only occur when income was above its equilibrium level, the latter being defined as the income level where planned saving is equal to planned investment. If, still using the assumptions of chapter III, it is now assumed that investment expenditures are a function of the level of income, investment as well as consumer expenditures will increase when the level of income rises. Further, if it is assumed that an increase in income results in increased investment expenditures without any lag, that is, the increated investment expenditure occurs within the period in which the income is earned, it will affect our previous conclusions in the same way as an increase in the marginal propensity to consume. An increase in the marginal propensity to consume tends to make unwanted accumulations or reductions in inventories more difficult to avoid, as was explained in chapter IV. The only difference introduced by the fact that the increased income is being spent for investment rather than for consumer goods is that some of the increased income may be used for the purchase of inventories. But this does not alter the previous conclusions. If the schedule of investment as a function of income is defined to include only investment in durable assets, then it is still true that no inventory accumulation can occur until the equilibrium level of income is exceeded. Moreover, as long as income and production are below the equilibrium level some liquidation of inventories will occur. On the other hand, if the investment function is defined to include planned additions to or reductions in inventory then it can be stated that these will only be fully realized at the equilibrium income level determined by the savings schedule and the schedule of investment including planned investment in inventory.

The next step is to introduce lags in expenditure. In chapter IV it was argued that a uniform lag in consumer expenditure made it easier to avoid unwanted accumulations or reductions in stocks. If investment expenditures arising out of increased income are also assumed to lag in a uniform manner the effect is exactly the same as the lag in consumer expenditures. The only difficulty is that they are less likely to do so. This is particularly true of large investment projects which often require a long period of advance planning and once begun, must be completed for reasons of economy even if in the meantime sales and income have fallen off. For these reasons the effects of lags in investment expenditures are somewhat uncertain.

The conclusions reached here are similar to the views of Mr. Hawtrey discussed in chapter II. Mr. Hawtrey argues that any planned investment in inventories will only be realized to the extent that the community absorbs cash. He assumes that any increase in income arising out of the production of goods for inventory will be immediately spent on either consumer or investment goods. If all of this income is spent no accumulation of inventory will occur. But since with rising incomes and sales individuals and business firms will find themselves in need of larger cash balances some of the income will be retained to provide these. This absorption of cash in Hawtrey's analysis is equivalent to the lag in the model here presented since cash balances are used to bridge the gap between the receipt and expenditure of income. I differ from Hawtrey in arguing that income saved and spent, either directly or indirectly, for investment goods may finance either inventories or other investment goods, whereas Hawtrey would seem to assume that it will all be spent for investment in durable assets .

Over the course of the business cycle the shape and stability of the savings and investment functions and the importance of lags in expenditure will largely determine the ease with which a planned inventory accumulation or liquidation can be achieved. In the initial stages of a recovery the large size of the marginal propensity to save and the length of time required to get major investment projects underway will make it easier for business firms to realize their plans for investing in inventory. Their task will be made more difficult if people become optimistic and start saving less so that the savings schedule shifts to the right. After allowing for lags their difficulties will be increased the more rapidly the investment function shifts upward. Similar conclusions apply to the downturn of a cycle: at such a time the increase in the marginal propensity to save and the lag involved in reducing investment expenditures will make it easier for firms to liquidate their inventories. It will be more difficult for them to do so if people become apprehensive and attempt to save a larger proportion of their income so that the savings schedule shifts to the left. This will also be true, after allowing for lags, if the investment schedule shifts downward. These conclusions are subject to the qualifications regarding the effects of price changes and expenditures on services discussed in chapters VI and VII.

This analysis suggests a possible explanation of the long lag found by Abramovitz between turning points in the volume of manufacturing inventories and the level of business activity.[17] As Abramovitz has argued, the lag is much too long to be explained entirely by the time required to reduce the rate of deliveries on outstanding orders and to reduce the manufacturer's own level of output. Sudden shifts in the saving and investment schedule at cyclical turning points would make it particularly difficult for business firms to avoid unwanted changes in their inventories at that time. It is also possible that some of the inventory accumulation that occurs after the downturn and some of the reduction in inventories that follows the upturn may be undertaken voluntarily.

CHAPTER NINE

SUMMARY AND CONCLUSIONS

ANALYSIS of a model of the economic system has provided a specification of the conditions under which a planned accumulation or liquidation of inventories can be achieved. Though an individual firm, acting alone, can easily accumulate or liquidate inventories, all firms acting together face a different problem. An individual firm can neglect the extent to which its own sales are dependent on its own output. But when all firms acting together are considered, this interdependence between sales and output is of prime importance. In a simplified model of the economic system it was shown that no accumulation of inventories will occur until income rises above an equilibrium level, defined as the income level where planned investment in durable assets is equal to planned savings. It was also shown that some liquidation of inventories will occur whenever income is below this equilibrium level. Though this conclusion was modified somewhat as various simplifying assumptions were abandoned it held up surprisingly well. The existence of lags in expenditure modify it somewhat, for lags make it easier for firms to carry out their plans for increasing or decreasing inventory. If income is rising at a uniform rate and there is a constant lag in expenditure the rate of saving will be increased above its normal level. In these circumstances inventories will be accumulated as soon as income rises above the equilibrium level determined by this higher short-run schedule of savings. If expenditures on services are important the average lag may be small, for money spent on services becomes available at once for re-expenditure. A further modification of this conclusion is necessary when price increases are used to defend declining inventory positions and when price reductions are used to clear surplus stocks.

If investment expenditures are related in a positive manner to the level of income, the above conclusion needs still further modification. The assumption that investment is related without lag to the level of income means that any shift in the investment or savings schedule will cause a larger change in the equilibrium level of income than would occur were investment independent of the level of income. This means that a larger increase in production will be needed to achieve an accumulation of stocks during an upswing, and a larger decrease in production will be necessary to secure some liquidation of stocks during a contraction. But it seems unlikely that lags between income and investment will be zero. The length of time needed to plan major investment projects and the expense and difficulty of stopping projects already underway make it likely that these lags will be long and irregular. Their effect will be similar to that of lags in consumers' spending: they will make it easier for business firms to realize their inventory investment plans.

In the short run, investment plans are closely related to business expectations which may be highly uncertain. Because of this the investment schedule is subject to sudden shifts which might offset the effects of these lags in spending. Thus, a sudden reduction in the rate at which new investment projects were undertaken might cause a sharp fall in the level of investment even though expenditure continued on projects already underway. These shifts are particularly likely to occur at cyclical turning points and thus may make it particularly difficult for firms to adjust their inventory position to the desired level at that time.

Analysis of the savings schedule suggests that the marginal propensity to save is usually large when the economy is operating at less than full employment. The larger the marginal propensity to save, the smaller the increase in spending resulting from any change in income and the easier it is to achieve any planned accumulation or liquidation of inventory. On the other hand, plans for changing the level of inventory can be made more difficult by shifts in the savings schedule. This would be the result if people tried to save more in periods of falling income and attempted to spend a larger proportion of their income in periods of expansion.

This study casts some doubt on Metzler's view that an inventory cycle may develop because business firms are unable to avoid undesired accumulations or reductions in stocks. These will not occur so long as production is increased or decreased sufficiently rapidly to keep income at its equilibrium level. Lags in both investment and consumer spending make this task easier. On the other hand, sudden shifts in the savings schedule or the investment schedule may make it difficult to avoid undesired changes in inventories. Such shifts may be particularly important at cyclical turning points and this may partially explain the finding of Abramovitz that inventories normally lag behind business activity at this time.

This analysis also supports the traditional view that the turning points in the business cycle may be caused by variations in investment in inventories, and that investment or disinvestment in inventories may be an important factor in reinforcing a cyclical expansion or contraction in income. Thus a decline in the rate of investment in inventories may precipitate a cyclical downturn. Similarly, a decline in the rate at which inventories are being liquidated may initiate a revival. Of course this would only be true if such changes in investment in inventories were not offset by opposite changes in other forms of investment. Hence they are, at best, a possible cause of cyclical turning points. If business firms reduce their inventories as their sales fall off and increase them again when they find their sales increasing, this alternate disinvestment and re-investment will reinforce the upward and downward course of cyclical activity. It can be argued that these effects tend to cancel out, that over a complete cycle they have no net effect on the total amount of income earned, but this will only be true if indirect effects are unimportant.

Changes in the value of total inventories may have effects on the course of the business cycle which are at least as important as changes in the volume of inventories. The value of total inventories will rise or fall with changes in the general level of prices and at times these changes may move in the opposite direction to changes in volume. Changes in inventory values are likely to have important multiplier effects on the rest of the economy which would be minimized if they were fully reflected in reported profits and if the inventory profits and losses they cause were completely discounted for policy purposes. There is evidence that in practice they are only partially reflected in reported profits and, even here, the windfall nature of these profits is not always recognized. For this reason a rise in inventory values may often be an important factor in reinforcing expansions in economic activity; a fall in inventory values may play an important part in accentuating cyclical contractions.

Changes in the total volume of inventories may conceal divergent movements in the stocks of particular commodities or stages of production. In general, an accumulation of stocks will occur whenever the consumption of a particular commodity declines below the level of production; a reduction in stocks will occur if production declines below the level of consumption. Thus the degree to which a commodity is subject to cyclical variations in demand and supply will determine the extent to which it participates in any accumulation or reduction in stocks. There is evidence that stocks of many primary materials accumulate during cyclical contractions and decline during periods of expansion. In farm and plantation products this counter-cyclical pattern of stocks is due to their relative stability in output in the face of a varying demand. Special study is needed to determine how the stocks of other commodities behave in relation to total inventories over the course of the cycle.

When inventories of a commodity accumulate during periods of contractions, the form in which these stocks are held, whether as raw materials or in a fabricated form, is uncertain; it will depend on the relative costs and risks involved in holding them in different forms and on the structure of orders throughout industry. In general, some increase in the proportion of finished goods might be expected in the initial stages of a downturn; some increase in the proportion of raw materials might be expected in the initial stages of an upturn.

A special theory of Keynes about the carrying costs of primary products which can be stored helps to explain the extreme variability of many primary product prices. According to this theory, when surplus stocks appear prices must fall to a level which will make it profitable for speculators to carry them until they can be reabsorbed by the market. If carrying charges are high in relation to price, the result may be an extreme fall in price. But contrary to the view of Keynes, improvement in demand seems to be more important than the stimulating effects of price reduction in inducing the removal of these surplus stocks. There is some evidence that these surplus stocks continue to pile up until the low point of the cycle is reached and begin to decline only when demand recovers. Because primary commodities are basic materials for a wide range of finished goods the rise and fall in their prices gradually spreads throughout the price system as they move into production channels. In fact, the entire pattern of cyclical price change seems to be closely related to inventory movements and inventory pricing policies.

Though this theoretical analysis has yielded valuable insights into the behaviour of inventories, there are many questions which can only be settled by a factual investigation. Is the minor cycle due to a deliberate attempt on the part of business firms to reduce their inventories or is it a result of a decline in the rate of inventory investment that is a natural result of a decline in the rate of output? Do business firms wish to keep their stocks in some fixed ratio to their sales or are they willing to allow substantial variations in their ratio of stocks to sales? Do inventory shortages create production bottlenecks during periods of expansion or are stocks usually adequate to allow an expansion to proceed at its own pace? Answers to some of these questions will be provided by this study of inventory fluctuations in the Canadian economy; answers to others must await further study.

PART II

INVENTORY FLUCTUATIONS IN CANADA, 1918 TO 1950

CHAPTER TEN

INVENTORY FLUCTUATIONS IN TEN MANUFACTURING
INDUSTRIES, 1918 TO 1950

THIS CHAPTER contains an analysis of the behaviour of inventories in ten manufacturing industries over the period 1918 to 1950. The industries selected were the ten largest ranked according to total value of inventory held in 1938. In that year these ten industries held about 39 per cent of all manufacturing inventories. The principal data available consist of the value of inventory on hand at the factory as reported to the Census of Industry for the company's fiscal year endings which in almost all industries was December 31. For the years 1931 to 1934 and 1941 to 1943 a breakdown of total inventory into raw materials, goods in process, and finished articles was available; monthly data on the value of inventories for most of the ten industries have been available since 1948.

In order to facilitate cyclical comparisons a series of monthly reference dates for Canadian business cycles was established for the period 1918 to 1950. These are given in Table 21. The criteria used in selecting these dates were similar to

TABLE 21

Monthly Reference Dates for Canadian Business Cycles, 1918 to 1950*

Peaks	Troughs
	March, 1919
October, 1920	January, 1922
October, 1923	December, 1924
July, 1929	March, 1933
October, 1937	July, 1938
September, 1944	February, 1946

* A peak may have occurred in 1918 but lack of monthly data makes it impossible to establish this.

those followed by the National Bureau of Economic Research.[1] It should be emphasized that these dates are highly tentative and much more work will be necessary if an authoritative set of reference dates is to be established. It will be noticed that the minor recessions of 1927 and 1949 in the United States did not appear in Canada. Some individual industries or products, particularly those dependent on the United States market, exhibited either one or both of these recessions but the effects of this on activity as a whole was too small to be labelled a recession. Over the period 1918 to 1938 the reference dates for Canada lag behind those of National Bureau's for the United States by an average of three months.

I. THE PULP AND PAPER INDUSTRY

In Canada this industry grew rapidly from the end of the first World War until

1929. After a period of stagnation in the early thirties, expansion was resumed at a somewhat slower rate in the late thirties and has continued into the postwar period. The industry's two principal products—newsprint (55 per cent), and woodpulp (23 per cent)—are sold predominantly in the United States market. In competitive structure the industry can be characterized as pure oligopoly which in turn confronts some elements of monopoly buying power in the sale of its products. Some of the smaller firms are controlled by publishers in the United States.

The rapid development of the industry in the twenties led to some excess capacity, a condition that was accentuated when demand fell off in the thirties. Because of the heavy capital investment required for a pulp and paper mill and the small number of firms in the industry, excess capacity led to an unstable price situation. As a result, there were frequent attempts during the thirties to restrict production and allocate demand as a method of maintaining prices. Even though supported by the provincial governments in Quebec and Ontario, none of these attempts succeeded in providing a stable pattern of prices and markets.[2] Newsprint, the industry's principal product, is usually sold under annual contracts. This removes from the industry some of the risk involved in carrying a large inventory.

The main part of the inventory carried at the mill, perhaps 80 per cent or more, consists of pulpwood; in addition, there are often small stocks of coal, sulphur, newsprint, and woodpulp. Pulpwood stocks at the mill usually reach a peak in the early autumn following the summer drive down the rivers. The level of mill stocks at year's end will reflect the annual consumption of the current year and the volume of pulpwood cut during the previous fall and winter. Because six months to a year normally elapse between the time the logs are cut and the time they are delivered to the mill, the level of stocks at the mill will not be adjusted quickly to changes in demand for the firm's products. A lag of one year in total inventory at the mill behind the change in annual pulpwood consumption is evident in 1921, 1922, 1925, 1930, 1934, 1938, and 1939. Because of this long lag, the volume of inventory at the mill may follow a counter-cyclical pattern during short cycles. Annual year-end stocks reached a peak in 1921, 1924, and 1938, all dates close to cyclical troughs. Over longer cycles the level of stocks conforms to the general cyclical pattern with a lag of about one year. Thus the volume of year-end inventories reported by pulp and paper mills increased somewhat irregularly from 1925 to 1930, declined from 1930 to 1933 and increased again from 1933 until 1938. If data on total stocks including undelivered pulpwood in the woods were available, it seems evident that this lag would be shorter. Statistics on logging employment provide some indication that the volume of logs in the bush shows little or no lag at turning points of the cycle.

The above data indicate that pulp and paper manufacturers have been able to adjust their stocks to an increase or decrease in sales after a lag of about one year. Even when sales were continuing to decline in the early thirties these firms were able, by cutting back production of new logs even more sharply, to achieve a substantial reduction in stocks on hand as well as some reduction in the ratio of stocks at year's end to the volume of sales during the year. This ratio has varied widely, although there has been a general decline over the period 1918 to 1950. It usually reaches a peak the year after a downturn and declines sharply in the year following an upturn; beyond this it shows no regular cyclical pattern.

It would appear probable that an increased demand for newsprint could be met fairly promptly in periods of depressed activity when the substantial amount of excess mill capacity can be readily utilized by drawing on mill stocks more rapidly. These stocks can be replenished fairly promptly by an increased rate of cutting in the woods and if necessary, by delivering logs by rail.

Investment in pulp and paper inventories (measured in constant prices) has usually reached a peak in the year following a downturn and a trough in the year following an upturn. For example, there were peaks in 1921, 1924, 1930, 1938, and 1940; there were throughs in 1922, 1925, and 1939. In short cycles such as the recessions of 1921, 1924, and 1938 this resulted in a completely counter-cyclical pattern. It seems likely that these changes were at least partially involuntary in nature. After a lag of about one year, the level of investment in inventories in the pulp and paper industry often changes very sharply. Thus, an investment of $12.8 million in 1921 was followed by a disinvestment of $9.3 million in 1922; and an investment of $18.3 million in 1930 was followed by a disinvestment of $12.7 million in 1931. In longer cyclical phases this reversal in direction would reinforce the contraction or expansion that was already under way.

In some instances the value of investment in pulp and paper inventories (the change in book value) moved in a different pattern or showed larger fluctuations than investment measured in constant prices. For example, the value series reached a peak in 1920 and began to decline in 1921. And during the contraction of the early thirties the value series showed much larger disinvestments than did the volume series. Thus the effects of rising and falling prices may sometimes offset the effects of changes in inventory volume and on other occasions may operate to reinforce these effects. This would be true to a smaller extent if selling prices were based on replacement costs and inventory profits were fully allowed for in determining the firm's dividend and investment policies. But it is doubtful if this is so. A majority of the firms use an average cost or first-in-first-out method of valuing inventory and about two-thirds stated that selling prices were based on actual as opposed to replacement costs. To the extent that the latter is true inventory profits would not appear with rising and falling prices.[3] Even if selling prices are partially based on replacement costs it is doubtful if inventory profits and losses are fully taken into account. An estimate of inventory revaluation prepared for twenty-six pulp and paper companies over the period 1936 to 1943 indicated that inventory profits estimated by customary methods would have amounted to 60 per cent of the companies' total net income over this period and would have been about one-third larger than total undistributed profits.[4]

While changes in inventories in this industry have been a factor in reinforcing cyclical fluctuations, they do not appear to have been an initiating factor. One exception occurred in the period 1949-50 when pulp and paper mills appear to have deliberately attempted to reduce the volume of stocks they carried. By December 1950 the value of total inventories was down 11 per cent over the same month two years earlier. This policy was reflected in sharply reduced employment in the logging industry; for the year ending June 1, 1950, it was down 42 per cent from the same period two years earlier. This loss of income to logging workers undoubtedly had a deflationary effect in this period and was a factor in the increased volume of unemployment in the winter of 1949-50.

II. The Non-ferrous Smelting and Refining Industry

Though there are ten firms in the non-ferrous smelting and refining industry it is dominated by three, the Aluminum Company of Canada, the International Nickel Company, and the Consolidated Mining and Smelting Company. A number of the smaller companies such as the Deloro Smelting and Refining Company which treats cobalt and Dominion Magnesium Limited which produces magnesium do not compete directly with any of the big three. All firms sell a large proportion of their output on the export market and most of them face some degree of competition. Competition has been severely restricted at times by international cartel agreements, particularly for copper, lead, zinc, and aluminum. The International Nickel Company has almost a world monopoly and has been able to maintain a stable monopoly price. Under cartel arrangements the maintenance of monopoly prices has often been accompanied by accumulations of stocks.[5]

Except for a sharp reduction in 1921 and 1922 and a minor decline in 1932 and 1933, Canadian output in this industry has moved almost continuously upward. A substantial accumulation of inventories occurred in 1920, but this had been eliminated by the end of 1922, principally by a sharp reduction in the output of copper and nickel. The decline in copper production may have reflected Canadian participation in a cartel arrangement. Some further accumulation of excess stocks occurred during the period 1929 to 1932 when the ratio of stocks to production increased from 21 per cent in 1929 to 37 per cent in 1932. However, with continued rapid growth caused by new developments in Canada and improved demand arising out of rearmament in Europe, the excess stocks were soon removed and by the end of 1936 the ratio of stocks to production had fallen to 11 per cent. The excess stocks of the mid thirties were held primarily in the form of finished products; finished goods inventory increased from 29 per cent of the total in 1931 to 63 per cent in 1932 and had only declined to 54 per cent by 1934. In the years of keen demand, 1941 and 1942, only 9 to 10 per cent of the industry's total inventory was held in the form of finished goods. Over the period 1918 to 1950 the stock-production ratio has fallen sharply.

Investment in inventories in the smelting and refining industry has behaved in such an irregular fashion that it is impossible to reach any firm conclusions about its cyclical pattern. This undoubtedly reflects the many special demand and supply factors affecting the industry. As a result of new discoveries and new technical developments there was a steady upward growth in the industry's output throughout the period and the normal cyclical pattern of industrial demand was disturbed by rearmament demands, particularly in the 1930's.

III. The Lumber Industry

The production of sawn lumber in Canada is a competitive industry. Over six thousand mills produced lumber in 1947 and, of these, the forty largest produced about 30 per cent of the industry's output. Export markets, particularly in the United States, are important and have usually taken from 40 to 50 per cent of the industry's output. In British Columbia lumber production is a year round business whereas in most other provinces it is predominantly seasonal. In eastern Canada logs are cut during the winter and sawn during the summer; production usually reaches a peak in June.

Over the period 1918 to 1939 both the volume and value of year-end inventories in this industry followed a pattern remarkably similar to annual output but with a lag of one year. After 1939 and particularly with the introduction of price control, inventories declined steadily until 1943 even though output remained at a fairly high level. Since then stocks have shown little variation, except for a decline in 1949 and 1950. In 1921, 1930, and 1938, all years in which output dropped, the volume of inventories increased substantially. After 1930 it declined sharply and continued to decline until two years after output had turned up. Despite a 68 per cent reduction in output between 1929 and 1932, the ratio of stocks to production increased sharply from 45 per cent in 1929 to 95 per cent in 1931 and 1932. This ratio declined sharply when output turned upward in 1933. The one year lag in the volume of inventory caused inventories to move in a counter-cyclical fashion in the short recessions of 1921 and 1938.

The stock-production ratio (the ratio of average beginning and year-end inventory in 1935-9 to the production of sawn lumber) followed a pattern almost the opposite of that shown by output for most of the period. Over the period as a whole the trend in this ratio was downward. Inventories amounted to only about 18 per cent of annual output in the four years 1947 to 1950 whereas in the years 1926 to 1929 this ratio averaged 50 per cent. When the ratio was at its highest in 1931 and 1932 there was about one year's production on hand in the form of logs or sawn lumber.

The lag in the volume of inventories behind output may be partially explained by the fact that logs in the woods are not reported as part of the mill's inventory. These stocks would likely decline with a shorter lag than those on hand at the mill. Furthermore, since lumber improves with seasoning there may be some incentive to hold larger stocks in relation to sales when demand slackens. There was no significant variation in the proportion of finished goods inventories held over the period 1931 to 1934.

Both the large amount of stocks and the marked degree of price fluctuation that occurs would tend to make this industry particularly subject to inventory profits and losses. Most of the mills surveyed reported that they used an average cost or specific item cost basis of inventory valuation—methods which reflect inventory profits if prices are based on replacement cost. On the other hand, nine out of twelve firms stated that actual cost had more weight than replacement cost in determining selling prices.

The pattern of investment in inventories in the lumber industry is similar to that of the pulp and paper industry but more irregular. There is the same lag at cyclical peaks with investment reaching peaks in 1921, 1924, and 1930, in each instance a year after the peak in business activity; there were also some lags at the lower turning point as indicated by the high rate of disinvestment in 1922 and 1939. But in other instances investment reached its trough in advance of the cycle, as in 1932, or at an unrelated date, as in 1927.

IV. THE TOBACCO INDUSTRY

The tobacco manufacturing industry in Canada is dominated by one large and one medium sized firm. In 1933 these two produced over 90 per cent of the industry's output. Because of its dominant size in a protected market, the largest firm, the Imperial Tobacco Company, has substantial monopoly power in buying and selling. It is the price leader and has followed a policy of maintaining stable prices on its finished products despite rather extreme fluctuations in raw tobacco prices.[6] Until 1933 tobacco was purchased directly from the growers under the barn buying system. There is evidence that competition during this period was limited by the policy of foreign buyers of buying under cover and by a practice of price leadership in setting buying prices. Since 1933, however, prices have been set by a joint committee consisting of three growers and three buyers. In addition, the growers' association has operated an acreage restriction scheme and at times has held substantial stocks of raw tobacco.[7]

Canada now produces about 98 per cent of her own requirements in raw tobacco and in recent years has exported about 15 per cent of her crop. Over the past thirty years imports have declined steadily in importance and exports have increased. A tariff of 40 cents per pound has discouraged imports but until the successful cultivation of flue-cured tobacco in the "new belt" during the late twenties and early thirties, imports continued to supply about one-half of Canada's requirements.

The inventory of the tobacco manufacturer will reflect year-to-year fluctuations in the size and value of the tobacco crop. Variations in planted acreage, output, and prices over the past thirty years have been marked and show some evidence of a cobweb pattern. Sudden changes in prices in one year have often been followed by sharp changes in planted acreage in the following year. Between 1917 and 1934 planted acreage went through four cycles whose average length was four and one-half years. Fluctuations in output have continued since that time but these have been affected to a considerable extent by acreage restrictions imposed by the growers' association and no longer clearly indicate a cobweb pattern. In addition, the development of the "new belt" introduced a downward rigidity in supply, for this area has fewer alternative crops.[8] This downward rigidity was illustrated in the early thirties when output continued to increase in the face of sharply declining prices. Though fluctuations in output have been marked, it is difficult to detect any regular relation of these to the business cycle. Yet it is possible that the practice of acreage regulation may introduce a positive relationship to the cycle in the future.

Tobacco manufacturers usually hold from two to three years' supply of tobacco so that it may be properly aged. Stocks of imported tobacco may be smaller than this since some of the imported tobacco is already cured. Finished tobacco products make up about 15 per cent of the total inventory. Changes in the value of inventory held by the manufacturer are reflected in farm income or imports and have at times moved in the opposite direction to the quantity of inventory. For example, during 1920 the value of manufacturers' inventory increased about $9 million and farm income from tobacco in the previous year increased by a similar amount, $10 million, as a large crop was sold to the manufacturer at favourable prices.[9] But with a still larger crop the following year prices collapsed, farm income from tobacco declined about $10 million, and the manufacturers' inventory was down by $5 million even though the volume was greater. In terms of its effect on the rest of the economy, the change in value of inventory may be more significant than changes in quantity. The rise and fall in the value of inventory, exerting its effect through farm income, would have an alternate expansionary and contractionary effect on the economy.

The total value of inventory held by the industry conformed to the major cycle of the thirties with a lag of about a year but has shown no regular relation to shorter cycles. In terms of volume a major accumulation occurred in 1920 and

1921 and this was gradually worked off over the following three years. Both stocks and output in the industry increased gradually from 1924 to 1929. In 1930 and 1931 a further substantial accumulation of inventory occurred despite a fairly sharp reduction in the output of tobacco products. Extensive plantings in the early thirties in the face of sharply declining farm prices undoubtedly encouraged the tobacco companies to carry larger inventories of raw materials. If they had not been willing to buy for stock, an even sharper fall in prices might have occurred because the manufacturers' policy of stable prices for the finished product does not allow the decline in the price of raw materials to stimulate increased consumption. The president of the Imperial Tobacco Company stated that as of May 1934 their company was holding about four to five million pounds more tobacco than they normally would. He stated that this had been purchased to help support the market but that it was also good tobacco and a profitable investment.[10] The company's vulnerability to public criticism may have caused it to take some steps to support the market. During this period the Ontario government also purchased substantial amounts of tobacco to help support prices. Because he carries from two to three years supply of tobacco, the manufacturer cannot quickly adjust his stocks to changes in demand. On the other hand, he seems to have been able to meet most increases in demand for finished products without delay.

No regular pattern is observable in the behaviour of investment in inventories in the tobacco industry. Variations in the size of the crop due to climatic conditions have combined with "cobweb" reactions in the size of the crop planted to produce a very irregular cyclical pattern of inventory investment. It seems doubtful that estimates of inventory profits have any significance in this industry. Most firms use either an average or a specific item cost basis of inventory evaluation and all firms stated that actual rather than replacement cost was important in determining selling price. The industry has been able to maintain remarkably stable profits despite severe fluctuations in raw tobacco prices: profits of the Imperial Tobacco Company declined by only about 3 per cent between 1929 and 1933; farm prices of tobacco fell more than 45 per cent over the same period.

V. The Petroleum Products Industry

In Canada the petroleum products industry, which refines crude oil into finished petroleum products, is dominated by three large firms and these three plus some smaller independents provide about 85 per cent of Canada's requirements. Until recently the industry was almost entirely dependent on imported crude oil but Canadian production has been increasing rapidly and in 1951 supplied about one-third of the industry's requirements. Imperial Oil is acknowledged to be the industry's price leader and competition has taken the form of advertising and the development of a large number of retail outlets.

The industry carries a large inventory of crude oil and finished products at the refinery; in addition, substantial inventories of finished products are maintained in marketing channels. Annual data on inventories at the refinery are available only for the period 1918 to 1950 and data on stocks in marketing channels have been available only since 1939. In 1950 the latter amounted to about one-third of the industry's total inventory.

Over the period 1918 to 1950 production of petroleum products has shown a marked upward trend. The only major interruption to this occurred in the depression of the thirties. The total volume of inventory held at the refinery has followed this growth closely and the ratio of stocks to production has remained remarkably stable over most of this period; the ratio has moved to a somewhat lower level in recent years. Inventories increased rapidly in 1929, jumping by well over 50 per cent, but this increase was necessary to restore the ratio of inventory to production to a normal level. The ratio had declined sharply in the late twenties as sales of the industry's products increased rapidly. With the decline in production which began in 1930 inventories were reduced without lag and the ratio of stocks to production remained fairly constant throughout the thirties. Variations in inventories in this industry cause similar changes in imports so that the direct effects on income in Canada are likely to be small. The data indicate that, over most of this period, this industry has been able to adjust its inventory fairly quickly to changes in sales. Over the period 1931 to 1934 the proportion of inventory held at the refinery in the form of finished products gradually increased from 49 per cent in 1931 to 59 per cent in 1934.

The cyclical pattern of investment in inventories has been variable. Prior to 1925 investment moved in an almost counter-cyclical pattern reaching peaks in 1921 and 1924 and a trough in 1923. Since that time investment has conformed positively to the cycle but has sometimes reached its peaks and troughs well ahead of the cycle in business activity. This was true of the trough in 1930 and the peak in 1935. But in both of these instances there was a later but smaller trough and peak in the year of the reference trough and peak. In the postwar period there was a deliberate reduction in inventories in 1949 despite the continued growth in output.

Since most of the firms in this industry use an average cost or first-in-first-out basis of inventory calculation, their reported profits would be affected substantially by price changes if prices were based on replacement costs. The firms surveyed were about equally divided in their opinion as to whether actual cost or replacement cost received the most weight in determining selling price. It seems probable that the rise and fall in the value of stocks on hand in this industry has exerted some net additional expansionary and contractionary effect on the economy.

VI. The Electrical Manufacturing Industry

Competitive conditions within the electrical manufacturing industry are extremely varied. It produces an exceedingly diverse range of articles—both heavy producer goods such as generators and transformers and a variety of consumer goods such as toasters, radios, and refrigerators. Some of the larger firms manufacture a wide range of items while others specialize in a few products or produce only components, such as condensers, for use in the manufacture of final products. For some products, such as radios, competition is keen; for others, such as large transformers, heavy generators, or telegraphic equipment, production is confined to a few firms. Most heavy electrical equipment as well as some parts for consumer goods are produced to the purchaser's specification under binding orders. The industry is a heavy importer of partially manufactured components for electrical equipment.

The ratio of stocks to production in the industry (the ratio of average beginning and year-end inventory to gross value of production) has followed a pattern which is markedly inverse to that of the industry's gross value of production, particularly from 1923 to 1938. From 1923 to 1929, a period of expanding output, this ratio declined from 35 to 19 per cent, then it increased to 46 per cent in 1933 and declined to 28 per cent in 1937. Correspondingly, the gross value of production in constant dollars declined $64 million in the second period and increased by $58 million in the third. On the other hand, during the war period, the ratio remained fairly constant at about 26 per cent in the face of rapidly increasing output.

Both the value and estimated volume of year-end inventories appear to follow corresponding changes in the volume and value of output without substantial lag. The 1929 turning point is a partial exception. In terms of estimated volume, year-end inventories increased 12 per cent from 1929 to 1930 whereas the industry's output was at about the same level in both years. On the other hand the volume of year-end inventories declined more sharply from 1937 to 1938 than did output. Although this suggests that the industry can adjust stocks to changes in sales without appreciable lag, the rise in the stock-production ratio noted above indicates that the industry is not willing or able to adjust its stocks completely when output falls. In 1920 and 1921 the industry was growing rapidly and both output and volume of inventories increased steadily through this period. Growth continued without interruption through the 1924 recession. In 1948 the volume of inventories declined by about 13 per cent, presumably because of the restrictions placed on imports of electrical equipment in November 1947. A further decline of 9 per cent occurred in 1949 despite a continued increase in output. This may have been a precautionary reduction in stocks initiated because of fear that the recession in the United States would spread to Canada.

The proportion of finished goods to total inventory increased steadily from 37 per cent in 1931 to 51 per cent in 1934. This changing proportion was almost entirely due to a reduction in the amount of raw materials held; the dollar value of finished goods inventory remained almost constant throughout this period. Thus the increase in the ratio of inventory to sales from 1931 to 1934 was almost entirely due to the holding of a larger ratio of finished goods.

The importance of inventory profits in this industry is likely to vary with the type of product. One might expect that the prices of goods produced to fill binding orders would be based on actual cost and that inventory profits or losses would be of negligible importance. On the other hand, inventory profits on goods produced for stock might be substantial, since the prices of non-ferrous metals, the industry's major material, are subject to wide variations. Of the firms surveyed in this industry, a majority reported the use of a specific item, average cost or first-in-first-out basis of inventory valuation. One larger firm reported the use of the last-in-first-out method. About one-half of the firms reported that replacement cost was the most important factor in determining selling prices.

With the exception of a lag shown in 1921 and another in 1929, (which resulted in a trough in 1922 and a peak in 1930) investment in inventories in the electrical manufacturing industry reached its peaks and troughs in the same years as business activity in general. Investment reached peaks in 1920 and 1937 and troughs in 1933 and 1938. Because of the rapid upward growth in the industry, investment in inventories did not register any effects from the recession of 1923-4.

VII. THE PRIMARY IRON AND STEEL INDUSTRY

The major part of Canada's primary iron and steel products are manufactured at three large plants while a number of smaller companies produce limited amounts of pig iron and steel. Canada now produces more than two-thirds of her own steel and exports a small amount. Imports of primary iron and steel, which before 1929 provided about one-half of Canada's requirements, now provide only about one-third. In addition to finished steel products, Canada imports substantial quantities of coal and iron ore for use in steel-making. The market for steel appears to be one of pure oligopoly with some local monopoly and the industry has pursued a policy of price stability in periods of depression, for prices declined less than 10 per cent between 1929 and 1933.

Steel plants stockpile substantial quantities of iron ore, coke, steel scrap, and limestone, may at times stockpile some pig and ingot, and hold a working inventory of finished steel products. Over the period 1918 to 1950 the industry's stock-production ratio (a ratio of average beginning and year-end inventory to annual output) showed a pattern almost the exact inverse of the gross value of output. This was particularly true in periods of subnormal activity. Thus the ratio increased from 23 per cent in 1929 to 99 per cent in 1932 and fell to 26 per cent by 1937. On the other hand, in periods of high activity the ratio has remained fairly stable even when production was rising rapidly. For example, from 1926 to 1929 the ratio only fell from 25 to 23 per cent even though output over this period increased about 75 per cent. One can conclude that the ratio falls to minimum working levels in periods of capacity or near capacity operation but increases sharply when production declines.

In recent years the value of year-end inventory has shown a consistent lag behind year-end sales. This was particularly marked at the downturn in 1929. Thus, although output declined by more than 25 per cent from 1929 to 1930, the value of year-end inventory increased from 1929 to 1930 by 29 per cent and showed its first decline in 1931. The effect of this lag of one year in the movement of year-end stocks produced a completely counter-cyclical movement in the short recession of 1938. Since prices have been fairly stable over most of this period the volume of inventory has followed a pattern similar to that of value. One exception to this occurred in the period 1920-1, when, as a result of the sharp fall in prices, the value of inventories declined along with output in 1921, whereas the volume of inventories continued to show an annual lag and increased in 1921. Both production and volume of inventory declined in 1924. Output rose slightly in 1925 but the decline in inventory continued into that year. The volume of inventory declined slightly in both 1949 and 1950 but the reduction in 1949 may have been deliberate, for it is one instance when a lag does not appear. The continuing fall in 1950 may have been involuntary, since sales and output increased sharply in the last half of 1950.

Data for the years 1941 to 1943 indicate that the proportion of finished goods held may be small in periods of intense activity. Finished goods amounted to only 12 per cent of the total inventory at the end of 1941 and 1942 but increased to 22 per cent in 1943 when output reached a peak and declined slightly. On the other hand, at the end of 1931, after output had been declining for two years, finished goods made up 33 per cent of the total. This percentage increased to 62 in 1932 and remained at about that level until 1934. This change was partly due to the conversion of materials on hand into finished goods inventory: between the end of 1931 and 1932 the stock of materials on hand was reduced about one-half whereas finished goods inventory increased some 45 per cent.

Reported profits in the iron and steel industry reflect some inventory profits and losses but it is doubtful if these are substantial. The industry's policy of price stability in periods of depression would tend to minimize inventory losses. Of the industry's major raw materials only the price of steel scrap declined substantially in the 1930's. Furthermore, one of the companies reported that a last-in-first-out basis of inventory valuation was used, and twelve that actual cost was the more important consideration in determining selling prices whereas only five stated replacement cost was the more important. Finally, a substantial proportion of the industry's output is produced to order. When prices are based on actual cost and goods are produced to order it is doubtful if reported profits reflect any element of inventory profit.

Though there have been some exceptions, the primary iron and steel industry has shown a pattern of investment in inventory which conforms to the cycle with a lag of one year. In some short cycles this has resulted in a counter-cyclical investment pattern. Thus, investment reached peaks in 1921 and 1938 and troughs in 1922 and 1939, moving counter to business activity in both instances. Investment also reached a peak in 1930, a year after the downturn of 1929. But in 1923 and 1924 the peaks and troughs in inventory investment showed no lag and a maximum rate of disinvestment was reached in 1932—a year ahead of the reference date. Steel output also reached a trough in 1932. In 1949 a very small decline in steel output was accompanied by a reduction in inventories of about 8 per cent.

VIII. THE AGRICULTURAL IMPLEMENTS INDUSTRY

Canada both imports and exports farm implements on an extensive scale. In recent years imports, chiefly from the United States, have supplied about 70 per cent of Canadian requirements. Canada's production is about equally divided between the domestic and export market. Formerly, most of Canada's exports went to the sterling area or to South America but in the past few years the United States has taken an increasing proportion of the total. The few large firms that dominate the market in both Canada and the United States have pursued a policy of maintaining prices in periods of reduced activity; prices in Canada declined only 2.5 per cent between 1929 and 1932.

Inventories in this industry follow a regular seasonal pattern reaching a low point in August or September and a peak between January and April. In addition to their factory inventories, the major Canadian companies hold extensive stocks of implements in wholesale channels; no data are available on the movement of these wholesale stocks though a survey in 1950 showed that they amount to about one-third of the industry's total inventory. Except for the year 1934 annual changes in the value of inventory held at the factory have followed changes in the gross value of production at cyclical turning points without lag. A lag of one year occurred in 1934 and a further exception, which will be discussed later, occurred in 1949. The estimated volume of inventories followed a pattern similar to that of value except for the period 1920-3. The volume of inventories reached a peak at the end of 1921, a year later than the peak in production, and then declined continuously until December 1924. Output rose sharply in 1923 and then declined slightly in 1924. Both the value and volume of inventories reached a peak in 1929 and declined thereafter. This suggests that manufacturers of farm implements are able to make some adjustment in their inventories fairly quickly in response to changes in sales. Their ability to do so may be helped by the fact that there is usually a seasonal accumulation of inventories in the latter part of the year, a time when the size and value of the current year's crop is already known. It is possible that this reduction in factory stocks could be offset by an opposite movement in the inventories held by these companies in wholesale channels. However, available data do not support this hypothesis. The total inventories of two large companies over the period 1928 to 1934 moved in about the same way as factory stocks.[11]

Although the level of stocks tends to move in the same direction as current production it does not vary so widely. As a result, the ratio of factory stocks to gross value of production in constant dollars shows marked variations. This ratio increased from 68 per cent in 1927 to 442 per cent in 1932. In the face of a severe decline in sales and output (production declined 86 per cent between 1929 and 1932) manufacturers apparently decided to maintain a high ratio of stock to sales rather than cease production almost completely. The need to keep key personnel together and to compete in bringing out new models of implements would favour such a policy. The proportion of finished goods to total inventory remained almost constant from 1931 to 1933 but declined from 75 per cent to 68 per cent as output and sales turned up in 1934.

Investment in inventories in the farm implements industry has not followed a regular cyclical pattern in the past. This may reflect the fact that the prosperity of the agricultural community sometimes follows a different pattern from industrial prosperity. Investment in inventories in this industry reached a peak in 1921, a year after the reference peak of 1920, and this was followed by heavy disinvestment in 1922. After that, investment in inventories increased slowly and steadily to reach a peak in 1929. This peak was followed by a heavy though fluctuating rate of disinvestment from 1930 to 1934. Investment then increased to reach a peak in 1937 and a subsequent trough in 1939. The disinvestment in 1939 accompanied a sharp decline in output, a decline for which there is no apparent explanation since both farm income and national income increased from 1938 to 1939.

In the postwar period investment in inventories reached a peak in 1946 and a trough in 1949. Since the heavy disinvestment in 1949 occurred in the face of rising output and sales it suggests a deliberate policy on the part of the industry to avoid being caught with excessive inventory in the event of a decline in sales. The current stock-production ratio is only about one-half as large as it was in the late twenties.

Some awareness of the problem of inventory profits has been shown in this industry. A representative of the International Harvester Company admitted before a House of Commons committee that the parent company in the United States had adopted a base-stock form of inventory valuation in 1916. Inventory was valued at 1916 prices from 1916 to 1921 and then written down to market. The company realized that inventory profits arising out of the increase, in prices during World War I might be lost in a subsequent price decline and hence they were not shown in the company's statement. An inventory reserve was built up again during the twenties and by 1929 the value of inventories on the balance sheet were understated to the extent of $40 million. This secret reserve was restored to profits in the period of declining prices 1929 to 1933. Since prices did not rise during the twenties the inventory reserve accumulated during this period was really a secret reserve built up to offset a possible loss of profits in case of a subsequent recession. Thus, while it is apparent that the company's executives had some concept of inventory profits it is not clear that they always distinguished these clearly from operating profits based on a comparison of current purchases and current sales. A similar policy was followed by the Canadian company before 1921 but not during the twenties.[12]

IX. The Fruit and Vegetables Preparations Industry

The fruit and vegetable preparations industry in Canada includes a few large, and a number of smaller firms producing canned fruits and vegetables, soups, infant foods, jams, jellies, pickles, fruit and vegetable juices, and fast frozen foods.[13] The larger firms sell their products under well-established brand names which give them some degree of monopoly power. Only the larger firms produce a full range of products and the degree of competition will vary somewhat among these different products. It has been alleged that competition is keenest in the canning of tomatoes;[14] since very little equipment is required, a number of small firms produce only this one product. The industry's products also compete with imported fruits and vegetables (both fresh and canned) throughout the year and with domestic fresh products in season.

The larger vegetable canners customarily purchase their produce under annual contracts with the growers. These contracts specify delivery dates, kinds of seed to be used, quantities to be accepted, and prices. In recent years provincial marketing legislation in Ontario and British Columbia has provided for negotiation of minimum prices on some products by committees of growers and canners. Variations in manufacturers' stocks in this industry will depend on advance commitments that have been made to purchase certain quantities of raw produce, and on current sales. Because contracts with growers are usually made in late winter or early spring the canner will not be able to reduce his output readily if sales fall off. Variations in crops both as a result of weather and planted acreage introduce an irregular variation into canners' stocks. In the case of annual crops the planted acreage of individual fruits or vegetables may change quickly from year to year. On the other hand, the supply of tree fruits, changes only very slowly in response to price. Several years are required to develop new orchards, and fruit from old trees may continue to be marketed despite adverse prices.

The trend of output in this industry has been markedly upward over the period 1918 to 1950, with major interruptions only in the early twenties and again in the early thirties. Though, in general, the volume of inventories has paralleled this growth, there were substantial accumulations of stocks in both the early twenties and early thirties. In the former instance all of the excessive accumulation occurred in 1920 when a large pack met declining sales in late 1920 and 1921. This surplus was worked off gradually over the next three years. In 1930 a very sharp accumulation of stocks occurred even though sales declined only moderately. Stocks increased further in 1931 and then declined steadily until the end of 1933. The 1930 pack was generally acknowledged in the trade to be excessive and large stocks were carried for a number of years thereafter. From 1930 to 1934, the largest firm in the industry, Canadian Canners, had almost a year's supply on hand when seeking orders for spring and summer delivery. This was almost double the amount held in 1929.[15] Canned goods are not marked with the year of pack and can be held in stock up to two years without any appreciable deterioration. Executives of the company estimated that annual carrying charges on this stock amounted to 10 per cent. However, they apparently made no concerted attempt to reduce the accumulation and they expressed the belief that a large carryover was necessary. Some of the smaller firms and growers claimed that the large carryover was used as a device to depress the market in an attempt to force smaller firms out of business. Another large company attempted to reduce the excessive stocks which resulted from an overpack in 1930 by cutting its total pack sharply in subsequent years. Despite this, in 1934 it still had substantial quantities of corn and tomatoes on hand that had been packed in 1931.[61] This would suggest that the large accumulation of stocks which occurred in 1930 was due to an overestimation of potential sales and that stocks remained high for a number of years, partly because canners failed to reduce their output sufficiently, and partly because of a deliberate policy of carrying larger stocks.

The seasonal nature of the industry's operations makes it peculiarly vulnerable to a decline in sales. Both in 1920 and 1930 the industry was forced to accumulate a substantial volume of inventory at a time when prices were falling. In addition to the loss incurred on the liquidation of these surplus stocks it seems probable that this industry would also show substantial inventory losses in a period of falling prices. Most of the firms surveyed reported the use of an average cost method of inventory accounting and a majority indicated that selling prices were based on current replacement cost.

Because favourable weather is important in determining the size of the annual crop of fruits and vegetables, investment peaks in this industry are likely to occur in years of exceptionally large crops such as 1920 and 1930, and investment troughs are likely to coincide with years of unfavourable weather. In addition, there may at times be some "cobweb" reactions on the part of growers to price changes. As a result investment in inventories in this industry has behaved in a rather irregular fashion and often fluctuates sharply from one year to another.

X. The Distilled Liquor Industry

The distilled liquor industry in Canada is dominated by a few large firms whose total sales of matured liquors in recent years have been about equally divided between the domestic and export market. In the domestic market matured liquor is sold only to the provincial liquor control boards who exercise some degree of control over the price charged by the manufacturer. These boards in turn set retail prices on liquor at levels which will yield maximum profits or, at least, a substantial revenue. The liquor is sold directly to the public through the provinces' own retail outlets and, in some provinces, to licensed drinking places. The industry also sells substantial quantities of industrial alcohol.

Since liquor improves with aging the industry generally carries large stocks of liquor, at various stages of maturity, equal to from 8 to 10 years' annual sales. Because of their large inventory, distillers can only adjust their inventory position very slowly to changes in sales. Data on stocks of liquor on hand as of March 31 are available over the period 1918 to 1950. According to these data stocks declined after World War I when restrictions were placed on the use of grain in the production of liquor but beginning in 1922 stocks increased slowly until 1924 and then more rapidly until 1930. In the following two years a further small increase occurred and thereafter stocks were allowed to decline until 1938. Since 1938 there has been an almost continuous increase. Thus, throughout the thirties the movement of stocks appears to have been counter-cyclical whereas during the twenties and the forties stocks moved in the same direction as economic activity generally. This must have been in large measure a matter of deliberate policy. The small increase in stocks between 1930 and 1932 could have been avoided by a sharper cut in production, for sales were well maintained during these years. Similarly the reduction in stocks after 1933 was probably deliberate although it may have been more rapid than expected in the late thirties for the ratio of stocks to sales fell sharply at that time. Throughout the post-war period there has been a steady accumulation of stocks and by March 31, 1950, manufacturers had restored their stocks to about nine years' sales at current levels. Though stocks cannot be adjusted readily to changes in sales the wide variations that have occurred in the stock-sales ratio suggest that an increased demand for liquor can be met readily by drawing on stocks on hand and replacing them at a later date.

Though liquor stocks moved in a counter-cyclical fashion during the thirties, the total value of inventory reported by distillers followed a slightly different pattern. The value of inventory continued its steady increase of the twenties until December 1930 and thereafter declined until 1938. The $30 million increase in inventories during the twenties followed by the $17 million decline during the thirties would exert an alternate expansionary and contractionary influence on the economy.

In terms of the volume of stocks, annual investment was negative following World War I, and the rate of disinvestment reached a peak in 1920. Subsequently investment became positive and showed a gradual increase until it reached a peak in 1930. After that date investment in distilled spirits fell off rapidly, becoming negative in 1933 and reaching a maximum rate of disinvestment in 1937. Since 1938, with the exception of one year, 1944, investment has been positive although it has fluctuated somewhat irregularly. The over-all pattern of investment appears to conform to major cyclical fluctuations with a long lag. Major changes in liquor legislation such as the adoption and subsequent abandonment of prohibition in the United States undoubtedly had an influence on the industry as well.

It is doubtful if inventory profits and losses have had an important effect on reported profits in this industry. Most of the firms surveyed used an average cost method of inventory valuation and eight out of ten firms reported that actual cost was more important than replacement cost in determining selling prices. It appears likely that the industry has sufficient monopoly power to maintain a fairly stable profit by basing selling prices on the actual cost of manufacturing.

SUMMARY

The ten industries discussed above, though not necessarily representative of total manufacturing, illustrate the diversity that characterizes inventory behaviour in different industries. In a number of these, a substantial accumulation of inventories occurs at the onset of a recession. In longer cycles this accumulation will be reduced in the course of the contraction so that the movement of total inventories, measured in physical volume, conforms to the cycle with a lag of about one year. In shorter cycles this lag will make the movement of stocks almost completely counter-cyclical. Such a pattern appears in pulp and paper, lumber, and iron and steel production. A number of other industries exhibit a similar pattern except that in the depression of the thirties the initial accumulation of 1930 continued well into the decade. Inventories were only reduced after expansion had set in and demand had revived. This was true in the tobacco, fruit and vegetable preparation, distilled liquor, and non-ferrous smelting and refining industries. In these the accumulation of stocks that occurred in the thirties seems to have been, at least in part, a matter of deliberate policy. In the remaining three, inventories usually followed production without lag at cyclical turning points; at least no lag is discernible in annual data. This may be related to the fact that all three industries—petroleum products, agricultural implements, and electrical apparatus and supplies—are heavy importers of raw materials.

In a number of industries, the ratio of stocks to production moved in a counter-cyclical fashion. This was particularly true of primary iron and steel, agricultural implements, and electrical apparatus and supplies. In the last two, this occurred despite the fact that the volume of inventories followed the movement of production without lag. In a number of other industries the stock-production ratio was counter-cyclical in short cycles and partially counter-cyclical in longer cycles. In these latter industries, this pattern appears to be due almost entirely to the lag of stocks behind production at cyclical turning points. Only in the case of petroleum products was there no cyclical pattern in this ratio.

Data on the proportion of finished goods to total inventory in the early thirties show that in most of these industries there was a tendency for this proportion to increase as the depression deepened. This would enable producers to meet readily any increase in demand that occurred as recovery set in, thus supporting the position of Hawtrey as opposed to that of Keynes.[17] This tendency was particularly noticeable in non-ferrous smelting and refining, electrical apparatus and supplies, and primary iron and steel. In almost all of the ten industries, finished goods made up a much larger proportion of the total inventory in the period 1931 to 1934 than it did in the period 1941 to 1943.

In two of the industries—tobacco and fruit and vegetable preparations—output and stocks were affected to a substantial extent by variations in planted acreage and in yields. Fluctuations in production, to some extent independent of the business cycle, caused stocks to move at times in an irregular fashion. The continued output of both products in the early thirties caused stocks to accumulate to a greater extent than would otherwise have occurred. In the case of fruit and vegetables the low prices which accompanied their accumulation helped stimulate consumption. In contrast, in the case of tobacco a monopoly policy of rigid prices on the finished product prevented increased consumption and the accumulation of stocks that occurred led to the formation of a growers' association and a deliberate restriction of output.

The movement of stocks in the majority of these ten industries tends to reinforce major cycles. On the other hand, the long lag results in a counter-cyclical movement of stocks that tends to alleviate the minor recession. The pattern is not completely uniform, however, and an important exception appears to have occurred during the slight weakening in activity of 1949-50. The pulp and paper, lumber, electrical apparatus, petroleum products, agricultural implements, and primary iron and steel industries all reduced their stocks in 1949, even though in most of these industries production continued to increase. This appears to be one clear instance where a planned reduction in inventories caused some slackening in economic activity.

Fluctuations in the prices of goods held in inventory tend to add to the effect of the movement in volume of inventory in major cycles but might moderate the counter-cyclical effect when it occurs in minor cycles. The effect of price changes would be minimized if all firms based their selling prices on current replacement costs and discounted the effects of inventory profits and losses completely. Though the evidence is scanty, in the ten industries studied this possibility did not appear typical. In industries such as tobacco, distilled liquor, primary iron and steel, and agricultural implements where there is a substantial degree of monopoly, prices of finished products appear to be set on the basis of long-run profit considerations and do not follow raw material prices at all closely.

CHAPTER ELEVEN

INVENTORY FLUCTUATIONS IN THE
CANADIAN ECONOMY

ANNUAL ESTIMATES of the volume and value of total business inventories in Canada are available for the period 1926 to 1950. A breakdown of this total by main industrial groups has been published for the value, but not for the volume, series.[1] However, the author has secured access to unpublished estimates of the latter, and has prepared annual estimates of both the value and volume of manufacturing, transportation, electric utility, and grain inventories for the period 1918 to 1925.[2] A measure of the relative importance of the inventories held by different industrial groups is given in Table 22.

Cyclical fluctuations in investment occur in both the volume of goods held in inventory and the value of total inventory. Production and employment are directly affected by fluctuations in the former; fluctuations in the latter often have no corresponding direct effects in production but are merely a reflection of the change in the level of prices. Fluctuation in investment in inventories in terms of volume is particularly important in non-agricultural industries. On the other hand, inventories on the farm and in the form of grain in commercial channels often fluctuate unpredictably as a result of good and bad harvests rather than planned changes in production. For this reason, when discussing

TABLE 22

Inventory Holdings by Industrial Groups, Canada, 1926 to 1950 Average

	1935-9 $ million	Per cent of total
Manufacturing	871	31.4
Retail trade	441	15.9
Wholesale trade	288	10.4
Transportation, communication and storage	76	2.7
Mining	36	1.3
Forestry	32	1.2
Construction	27	1.0
Public utilities	16	.6
Miscellaneous	22	.8
Total non-agricultural	1,809	65.3
Grain in commercial channels	265	9.5
Farm	698	25.2
Total	2,772	100.0

SOURCE: Dominion Bureau of Statistics, unpublished data.

changes in the volume of goods held in inventory, it is necessary to concentrate mainly on non-agricultural inventories.

In addition to these direct effects, fluctuations in investment for both the volume and value of inventory may have indirect or multiplier effects on the economy, in which changes in value may be as important as changes in volume. In the following discussion, the term investment in inventories will refer to changes in the estimated volume of inventories, the term value of investment in inventories will refer to the change in current or book value of inventories.

As a long-run source of demand, investment in inventories has been of minor importance in Canada. Thus, over the period 1926 to 1950 only 1.2 per cent of Canada's gross national product took the form of goods added to inventory. During this same period investment in inventories amounted to only 8.3 per cent of total gross private investment in Canada, an amount equal to about two-fifths of the volume of new residential construction. The significance of inventory investment was reduced during this period by a decline in the ratio of total inventories to gross national product. This ratio fell from about 45 per cent in the period 1926 to 1929 to around 36 per cent in the period 1947 to 1950. Almost all of this decline is due to a reduction in the proportion of inventories held on the farm or as grain in commercial channels. The ratio of non-agricultural inventories to gross national product was about the same in both periods. However, even if the ratio of total inventories to gross national product had remained constant over this period, investment in inventories would only have accounted for 1.5 per cent of the total production of goods and services.

Though unimportant as a long-run source of demand, fluctuations in inventories are an important cause of cyclical expansions and contractions in the level

TABLE 23

Changes in Investment as a Percentage of Changes in Gross National Product, Canada, Periods of Expansion and Contraction, 1926 to 1950 (the War Years 1941 to 1945 Excepted) *

	4 Exp.	2 Cont.	Cycle	1926-29	1929-33	1933-37	1937-38	1938-40	1946-50
				Per cent					
Total durable assets	37.2	64.9	44.6	56.2	63.1	25.6	—136	12.5	56.6
Residential construction	5.6	9.4	6.6	2.1	8.5	6.0	— 52	2.1	10.5
Non-residential construction	12.7	24.2	15.7	25.4	23.0	6.7	— 60	2.5	19.3
Machinery and equipment	18.9	32.3	22.4	28.7	31.6	12.9	— 24	7.9	26.8
Total inventories	10.0	5.3	8.8	— 8.6	11.2	11.2	368	14.5	14.3
Non-agricultural	5.8	22.6	10.1	0.0	13.7	13.2	—532	8.1	— 3.7
Manufacturing	4.4	8.9	5.6	— 0.2	6.2	7.3	—160	4.5	2.1
Retail and wholesale	0.0	8.7	2.3	— 2.3	5.9	3.6	—168	0.1	— 2.9
Grain and farm	4.2	—17.3	— 1.3	— 8.6	— 2.5	— 2.0	900	6.4	18.0

* All data used were estimated in 1935-9 values.

SOURCE: Canada, Dominion Bureau of Statistics, unpublished data, and *National Accounts: Income and Expenditure, 1926-1950* (Ottawa, 1952).

of income, as Table 23 illustrates. In this table, changes in the level of investment between the peak and trough of a cycle are expressed as a percentage of the change in the level of gross national product during the same period. This means that if there was an investment in inventories of 100 in the peak year and a disinvestment of 60 in the trough year the decline in the level of investment in inventories would be 160. If gross national product fell by 800 between this peak and trough, the decline in investment in inventories would amount to 20 per cent of the total fall in gross national product.

Table 23 shows that over the period 1926 to 1950 fluctuations in inventories have accounted for 8.8 per cent of the change in gross national product. This is only about one-fifth as large as the change in total investment in durable assets. Since grain and farm inventories moved in a counter-cyclical manner, the change in non-agricultural inventories was slightly larger than this and it accounted for 10.1 per cent of the change in gross national product. Manufacturing inventories accounted for 5.6 per cent of the change in gross national product and retail and wholesale inventories for 2.3 per cent. These data indicate that in Canada investment in inventories has been less important as a cause of cyclical fluctuations in income than it has been in the United States. Abramovitz found that for five business cycles between 1919 and 1938 in the United States net changes in inventories accounted for about 32 per cent of the cyclical variation in gross national product.[3]

Why have inventory fluctuations been less important in Canada than in the United States? One reason is that minor cycles or recessions have occurred less frequently. The minor recessions of 1927 and 1949 were both absent in Canada. This would reduce the average importance of inventory fluctuations, for Abramovitz has shown that the shorter the cycle the greater the importance of inventory fluctuations.[4] But inventory fluctuations in Canada seem less important even in major cycles; for in the period from 1929 to 1937 this difference is still present although it is less pronounced. In the contraction from 1929 to 1937 investment in inventories accounted for 11 per cent of the decline in gross national product in Canada and 17 per cent in the United States. In the subsequent expansion the corresponding percentages are 11 for Canada and 20 for the United States. Some of this difference may be due to the fact that business firms in Canada are willing to countenance a greater rise in the ratio of stock to sales during a contraction than are their counterparts in the United States. In Canada this ratio increased from 46 to 62 per cent between 1929 and 1933 whereas during this same period in the United States it increased only from 37 to 45 per cent. The difference also undoubtedly reflects the greater tendency of Canadian investment in inventories to lead or lag rather than coincide with business activity at cyclical turning points.

An examination of annual fluctuations in investment in inventory reveals that their positive effects are often concentrated in a few years. In some years these effects are very large. Thus, between 1949 and 1950 some 72 per cent of the increase in gross national product took the form of an increased rate of investment in inventories. On the other hand, investment in inventories may often move in the opposite direction to the level of gross national product. Thus for the period 1926 to 1950 as a whole, the change in investment in inventories moved counter to the change in gross national product in 11 out of the 24 year-to-year changes. Though some of this irregularity is due to variations in the size of the western grain crop, the pattern is also present to a lesser degree in non-agricultural inventories.

These data also show that fluctuations in investment in non-agricultural inventories have been important in reinforcing contractions and expansions in gross national product and in some instances may explain cyclical turning points. Thus between 1929 and 1930 the decline in investment in non-agricultural inventories amounted to about one-half of the decline in gross national product. But in the following two years, though this series continued to fall, it accounted for a much smaller proportion of the decline in gross national product, only 15 per cent from 1930 to 1931 and 20 per cent from 1931 to 1932. In 1933 there was a substantial decline in the rate at which non-agricultural inventories were being liquidated and this may have contributed to the rise in activity that occurred in March 1933. In the period from 1933 to 1937 investment in non-agricultural inventories was never a major factor but it increased throughout this period and thus helped to reinforce the expansion. A sharp decline in the rate of investment occurred in 1938 and this must have been an important factor in reinforcing the recession in industrial activity that occurred at that time. In the post-war period investment was high in 1946 and 1947. In 1948 a substantial decline in the rate of inventory accumulation set in but caused no slackening in the growth of economic activity. Thus a decline in investment may have little effect if other expenditure forces are sufficiently strong.

Investment in non-agricultural inventories shows no consistent timing pattern at cyclical turning points. In the earlier period from 1919 to 1925, data (available for only three industries—manufacturing, railways and public utilities) show a lag of about one year; peaks appeared in 1921 and 1924 and troughs in 1922 and 1925. In 1929, 1937, and 1938 peaks and troughs coincided with those of business activity as a whole, although the peak in 1929 followed an earlier and higher peak in 1927. But its trough in 1932 preceded the general upturn by about one year. In the post-war period investment reached a peak in 1946, declined to a trough in 1948 and reached another peak in 1951, whereas total output continued upward throughout this entire period. In contrast, Abramovitz found that in the United States investment in inventories tends neither to lead nor to lag behind the turning points of business cycles.

Thus far, no distinction has been made between voluntary and involuntary accumulations of inventory. In fact, no precise distinction can be made. Despite the sharp drop in the rate of inventory investment in 1930, a small addition to inventories did occur in that year—the result of a substantial accumulation at the manufacturing level which was not completely offset by declines in other sectors. This may have been involuntary in the sense that manufacturers found it difficult to reduce production and new purchases of materials rapidly enough to avoid some inventory accumulation. In view of the widespread optimism that prevailed in the late twenties, it is quite possible that manufacturers at first underestimated the seriousness of the decline in activity with which they were faced, and for that reason allowed their inventory to accumulate in the mistaken view that an increase in demand would soon rid them of any surplus.

Fluctuations in investment in respect to the value of total inventories have followed a pattern that is rather similar to that of the volume of non-agricultural inventories. These fluctuations played a causal role at some turning points and helped to reinforce expansions and contractions in activity. Their relative importance in the latter respect often varied widely at different stages of the cycle. In both

CHART 3

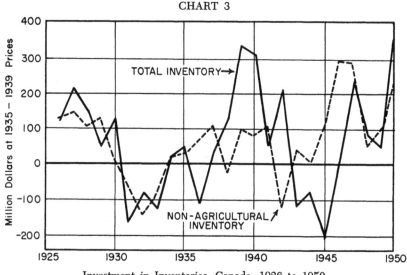

Investment in Inventories, Canada, 1926 to 1950

1928 and 1929 the value of investment in inventories declined moderately thus acting as a drag on the growth in economic activity; in 1930 it fell so sharply that it reached a cyclical trough in that year. Between 1929 and 1930 the decline in the value of investment in inventories amounted to about two-thirds of the decline in the value of gross national product. Thus it was an important factor in starting business on its downward course. But for the continued fall in income during the next two and one-half years, declines in other forms of spending were of much greater importance. Indeed the value of the investment in inventories reached a trough in 1930 and thereafter began to rise thus acting to check the fall in income rather than accelerate it. In 1933 the value increased sharply and, if it did not cause the upturn that occurred in that year, it at least contributed to that which followed. But in 1935 and 1936 the value declined and thus acted as a drag on recovery throughout these two years. This decline was due to the liquidation of the large stocks of wheat that had been built up during the early thirties. Annual data are not sufficiently precise to indicate what part inventories played in the downturn of 1937-8 but they do show that the decline in value between 1937 and 1938 accounted for a large part of the decline in the value of gross national product. Further, a rise in the value of inventory investment accounted for a major part of the increase in the value of output that occurred in 1939. However, the continued rise in gross national product in the following years was due to other expenditure forces. In the post-war period large increases in the value of investment in inventories occurred in 1946, 1947, and 1950, and substantial declines occurred in 1948 and 1949. Despite such fluctuating support, the level of activity in Canada has remained almost uniformly high throughout this period. Competition for investment funds and resources has been so keen that any reduction in the value of investment in inventories has been quickly replaced by other forms of expenditure.

There is reason to believe that the value of investment in inventories may be an important factor in aggravating inflation and deflation. The relation is one of both cause and effect. A rise in prices leads to an increase in the value of inventory and if this increase is financed out of additional bank loans the spending of these funds leads to a further rise in prices. The opposite is true in periods of falling prices. If a decline in inventory values leads to the paying off of bank loans, this withdrawal of funds from circulation will contribute to a further decline in prices. Table 24 gives some support to this thesis. The data presented there show that in most periods the volume of bank loans and the value of total inventories have moved in the same direction.

TABLE 24

Changes in Public Loans of the Chartered Banks and Changes in the Value of Inventories, Canada, 1926 to 1950

Dec. to Dec.	Current public loans chartered banks	Value of total inventory *
	Million dollars	
1926-29	433	559
1929-33	—505	—870
1933-37	—149	339
1938-41	278	886
1945-48	850	2,304
1948-50	574	1,140

* Excludes farm inventory.

SOURCE: Bank of Canada, *Statistical Summary, 1946 Supplement; Canadian Statistical Review;* and *National Accounts: Income and Expenditure 1926 to 1950* (Ottawa, 1952).

While at times the inflationary or deflationary impetus that the change in inventory values gives to the economy may be undesirable, at other times it may serve a valuable purpose. Inventories are a type of asset that commercial banks will readily finance. During periods of recovery, a rise in inventory values may facilitate an expansion of bank loans thus supplying the economy with the additional money required by a higher level of activity. If inventories were always carried at fixed values the banks might have difficulty finding a sufficient supply of suitable assets to finance during a period of recovery. Thus recovery might be hampered by a lack of elasticity in the supply of money.

Manufacturing inventories account for about 48 per cent of all non-agricultural inventory holdings in the Canadian economy. On the average, manufacturers hold from three to three and one-half months' production in stock and of this from 30 to 40 per cent in finished goods.

With one major exception, the value of year-end manufacturing inventories moved in the same direction as annual output over the period 1918 to 1950. The major exception occurred in 1923-4 when the value of manufacturing inventories continued to rise throughout the recession of 1924. Both the value of output and inventory reached a trough in 1922. However, the value of output, after a substantial rise in 1923, showed a mild decline in 1924, while the value of inventory showed a continuous rise from 1922 to 1924. The 1924 decline was reflected in inventory value only by an increase in the rate of accumulation.

Since the peaks and troughs in manufacturing inventory occur at the end rather than at the beginning of the years in which output reaches its peaks and troughs, a lag of some six months behind output is indicated. Abramovitz found a similar lag for the value of manufacturing inventories in the United States.[5]

CHART 4

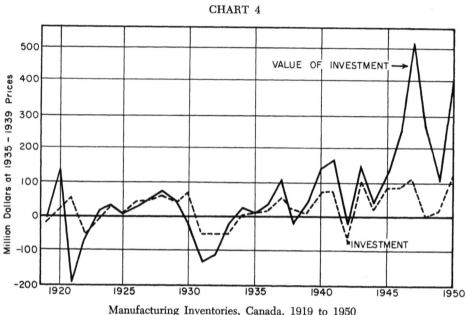

Manufacturing Inventories, Canada, 1919 to 1950
Investment and Value of Investment

The estimated volume of manufacturing inventory shows evidence of a much longer lag at major turning points. A comparison of year-end peaks and troughs in the volume of inventory with monthly turning points in the business cycle reveals an average lag of 15 months for five turning points between 1919 and 1937. Like the value series, the year-end volumes of inventories skip the recession of 1924, and the 1938 recession also. The behaviour of manufacturing inventories was different in each of these recessions. The year 1924 was marked by a rapid growth in inventory; inventories increased by 7 per cent in 1924 whereas they had declined 2 per cent in the preceding year. In contrast, 1938 was marked by a sharp drop in the rate of inventory accumulation; the volume of inventories increased only 3 per cent during 1938 whereas they had increased by 9 per cent in 1937. Thus, in Canada, manufacturing inventories have shown no consistent relation to the minor cycle.

In the case of the volume of manufacturing inventory, the annual rate of investment has typically reached a peak either in the same year as the peak in business activity or in the year following. Thus peak rates of investment were reached in 1921, 1930, and 1937. Further, troughs in the rate of investment were often reached in the year immediately following a peak. This was true in 1922 and 1925 and was substantially true in 1931 and 1938. All this suggests that part of the accumulation in these years of peak investment was involuntary and the subsequent sharp drop in the rate of investment was due to an effort to work off these surplus stocks.

The value of investment in manufacturing inventory is strongly influenced by the pattern of price changes and shows no tendency either to lead or to lag turning points in activity generally. Investment in terms of value of inventory, reached a peak in 1920 and 1937, both peak years in the business cycle, showed a lag of one year in 1924, and a lead of one year in 1928. Maximum rates of disinvestment were reached in 1921, 1931 (and 1932), and in 1938. In the post-war period the rise and fall in the rate of investment in manufacturing inventories shows little relation to a business cycle pattern. Activity continued high throughout this period despite a rise and fall in the value of investment in inventory.

A breakdown of the total manufacturing inventory into raw materials, goods in process, and supplies on the one hand, and finished goods on the other, provide some indication of the comparative behaviour of these different inventory categories over the business cycle. Such a breakdown is available for the years 1931 to 1934 and 1941 to 1943. These data are presented in Table 25 in the form of ratios of inventory to the average gross value of manufacturing production in the current and succeeding year. A basis for judging these data is provided by the behaviour of the corresponding ratio for total manufacturing

TABLE 25

Ratio of Raw Material and Goods in Process and of Finished Goods Inventory to the Average
Gross Value of Manufacturing Production in the Current and Succeeding Year,
Canada, 1931 to 1934 and 1941 to 1943

	Ratio of inventory of raw materials and goods in process to gross value of production	Ratio of inventory of finished goods to gross value of production
	Per cent	
1931	18.7	12.3
1932	17.2	13.0
1933	15.2	11.0
1934	13.4	10.2
1941	13.6	5.6
1942	13.4	5.0
1943	15.2	5.9

SOURCE: Canada, Dominion Bureau of Statistics, *The Manufacturing Industries of Canada, Annual Reports* (Ottawa, 1930-5, 1940-4).

inventory. This ratio increased from a low point of 22.1 per cent in December 1928 to a high of 31.0 in December 1931, and then declined to a low point in 1936. The ratio for total inventory in 1941 was 19.2, about the same as the ratio in 1936, 19.7 per cent. If the ratios in 1941 can be taken as a measure of what is typical in periods of high employment, then both raw material and finished goods inventory were high in relation to production in 1931. As the depression deepened the ratio of finished goods inventory remained high but the proportion of raw materials inventory declined steadily. This suggests the following explanation. In the early stages of the depression business firms accumulated excessive stocks of both raw materials and finished goods, but as the depression continued these raw materials were gradually converted into finished goods.

The proportion of total inventory held in the form of finished goods was substantially higher in the period from 1931 to 1934 than it was in the period from 1941 to 1943. In the former—a time of severely depressed activity—an average of 42 per cent of total inventory was held in the form of finished goods. In the years of much higher activity—1941 to 1943—only 28 per cent of total manufacturing inventory was held in the form of finished goods. This pattern was true for most manufacturing industries.

Both the higher ratio of inventory to production and the increased proportion of finished goods to total inventory carried by manufacturers in years of depressed activity support the view of Hawtrey that increased production can begin at all stages of production simultaneously. When the ratio of inventory to production is well above the ratio customarily carried at peak levels of activity, manufacturers should have ample stocks to allow them to begin increased production without delay. Further, when finished goods inventory at all stages is ample, increased orders for materials can be filled promptly.

The estimated year-end volumes of wholesale inventories generally reach their peaks and troughs in the same year as the monthly turning points of the business cycle. Thus they reached peaks in 1929 and 1937 and troughs in 1933 and 1938. Investment in inventories has been positive in most years of expansion and negative during most years of contraction. Exceptions occurred in 1928, when wholesale inventories declined about 4.5 per cent in volume, and in 1940, when a small decline occurred. Over the period 1926 to 1950 the rate of investment in wholesale inventories fluctuated rather irregularly. The rate of investment was high in 1926, 1936, 1939, 1946, and 1950. Some of these years are located near the beginning of a period of expansion, others near the end. In most instances the peak rate of investment was reached before the end of the expansion period so that investment had begun to decline before the downturn occurred. In the one long period of contraction during this period, 1929 to 1933, wholesale inventories, after a fall of about 1 per cent in 1930, declined steadily at the rate of 9 to 10 per cent each year.

In the main, the estimated year-end volume of inventories in retail trade reaches peaks and troughs in the same year as activity generally. In the period 1925 to 1950, peaks occurred in 1929 and 1937 and troughs in 1934 and 1938. Retail inventories declined steadily throughout the war and increased substantially after the war's end. With a few exceptions investment in retail inventories proceeded at a steadier pace than was true of wholesale inventories. There is no evidence that investment in retail inventories begins to decline in advance of a downturn. In the post-war period retail inventories increased about 20 per cent in volume in both 1946 and 1947, remained almost unchanged in 1948, and increased about 10 per cent in both 1949 and 1950. The failure of inventories to rise appreciably during 1948 may have been due to the import restrictions imposed on a wide range of consumers' goods in November 1947.

Data on ratios of stocks to sales are available for seven large department stores over the period 1924 to 1933 and for all chain stores for the period 1934 to 1949.[6] The ratio of year-end stocks to annual sales in the department stores increased slightly during the contraction from 1929 to 1933 but the rise was very small. Over the period as a whole, year-end inventories varied within the range of 15.3 to 16.7 per cent of annual sales. The ratio of stocks to sales in chain stores remained relatively constant from 1934 to 1940 and then declined substantially during the war. This ratio increased a little after the war's end but in 1949 stocks were still only equal to about 12 per cent of annual sales whereas between 1934 and 1940 they had averaged about 14.5 per cent. Apart from war-time shortages, this evidence suggests that retailers have been able to avoid any substantial variation in their stock-sales ratio.

Data on inventories of logging companies have been available only since 1944; prior to that time estimates were based on an index of logging employment during the last five months of each year. This assumes that year-end logging inventories will be composed entirely of logs cut during the preceding five months. This is a reasonable assumption since logs are cut mainly during the winter months and are moved out of the woods when the river opens up in the spring.

Estimated on this basis, the volume of logging inventories follows without any lag the wide fluctuations in annual output. Fluctuations in logging inventories have been large in amplitude. Inventories declined by over 40 per cent between 1929 and 1930 and by 1932 they were less than one-third of their 1929 level. Between 1932 and 1933 they increased two and one-half times.

In chapter X it was pointed out that the variation in logging inventories would tend to offset the lag at turning points shown by inventories in the lumber and pulp and paper industries. Any increase or decrease in activity in these two industries is reflected in the logging industry almost at once. When inventories for the three groups (logging, pulp and paper, and lumber) are combined, total inventories still show a lag in 1930 but the lag in 1937-8 disappears; total inventories for the three groups declined $15 million between 1937 and 1938, whereas for lumber and pulp and paper, inventories increased by $10 million. Moreover, the addition of logging inventories reduces by one-third the accumulation shown by the other two industries in 1930 and results in a much sharper increase in 1934. The sharp reduction in logging inventories in the fall of 1949 was an important cause of the rise in unemployment that occurred in the winter of 1949-50.

In the transportation, communication, and storage group, steam railways hold about 85 per cent of the total inventory. Railway inventories consists mainly of coal and construction materials. Inventories in this group of industries rise and fall with major expansions and contractions in activity but their behaviour is often irregular. The value and volume of railway inventories reached a peak in 1921, a year after the general downturn, but in 1923 and 1929 they reached a peak in the same year as activity generally. After 1923 railway inventories continued to decline until 1926, two years after the business cycle trough of 1924. Again, in the 1930's railway inventories reached a trough in 1934 and then fluctuated irregularly until 1939; no substantial rise in inventories occurred until 1940. The failure of railway inventories to rise more in the late thirties can be attributed to the low level of railway earnings and traffic in that period, owing, in part, to the small grain crops in the West. In the post-war period, railway inventories reached a peak in 1948 and declined sharply in 1949.

Over the period 1926 to 1950 Canadian mining inventories show no regular pattern of behaviour in relation to the business cycle. The volume of mining inventories increased by about 19 per cent in 1929, declined slightly in 1930 and after a further increase of 9 per cent reached a peak in December 1931. There is no obvious explanation for this late peak; production had declined by about 12 per cent between 1929 and 1931 so that stocks were unusually large in relation to sales at that time. In 1932 inventories declined by about 18 per cent. Thereafter they increased at an irregular rate until 1942. After a decline during the latter part of the war period they increased rapidly during 1946 and have fluctuated within rather narrow limits since that time.

The importance of gold mining inventories may account for some of this irregularity, for gold production often follows a counter-cyclical pattern. It increased rapidly in the early thirties, remained almost constant from 1932 to 1934, and then increased rapidly until production was reduced in 1942 to release labour for war purposes.

The chief inventory holders in the public utility field are central electric stations. Because many electrical power companies do some or all of their own construction they often carry substantial inventories of construction materials, and since it often takes several years to complete power projects that are under construction when a downturn begins, inventories in this industry fluctuate irregularly and often show a long lag at cyclical turning points. Similarly, a long period of planning is required before new projects get under way. Thus both the volume and value of year-end inventories in this industry reached a peak in 1931, a year in which net additions to installed power also reached a peak. After 1931 a decline set in, which continued until 1936 for the value of inventory, and until 1937 for the estimated volume of inventory. Except for a decline in the peak war years, inventories in this industry have risen steadily since that date. With the extensive construction of power projects in the postwar period there has been a rapid rise in inventories in this industry: the estimated volume of public utility inventories increased by 27 per cent in 1945, 29 per cent in 1946, 43 per cent in 1947, and 32 per cent in 1948. In the period before 1930 there were large temporary inventory accumulations in 1923-4 and in 1927. Both of these appear to have been related to major construction projects that were under way at that time.

For inventories of grain on the farm or in commercial channels the national income estimates in Canada include the annual physical change valued at annual average prices. This gives the most accurate measure of that part of the current production of goods and services which has been added to grain inventories and for that reason is the correct total to include in gross national expenditure. However, in assessing the economic effects of this change in inventories the increase or decrease in the market value of grain held in inventory at the beginning and end of the year is also important.

Most of the grain on hand at the beginning of the year is marketed during the first eight months of the year at the prices prevailing during that period. A large proportion of the wheat and a smaller proportion of the coarse grains are exported. During the remainder of the year stocks are built up again as the crop is harvested. If prices prevailing in the latter part of the year are higher than prices at the beginning of the year this will be reflected in increased payments to the farmer as grain is delivered to the elevators and sold. Thus, almost the full rise in market value of year-end inventories may be reflected in higher income payments if prices have risen, or in a reduction in income payments if prices have fallen. Since grain in commercial channels is normally financed by

CHART 5

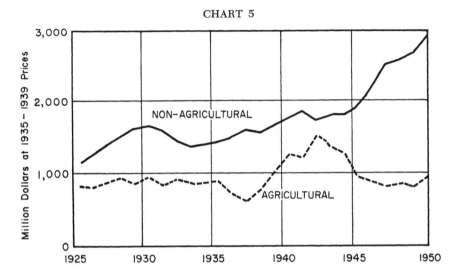

NOTE : Agricultural= Farm Inventory plus grain in Commercial Channels.

Value of Agricultural and Non-Agricultural Inventory, Canada, 1926 to 1950
(end of year)

means of bank loans, this rise or fall in the value of inventory will have a corresponding inflationary or deflationary effect on the rest of the economy. In some instances values and quantities may move in different directions. Thus if prices rise sharply with short crops both in Canada and abroad the market value of grain held at the end of the year may be up even though the quantity of grain held has declined. In these circumstances the change in the value of grain held is more significant than the change in quantity. Farm incomes increase correspondingly and increased spending by farmers follows.[7]

This conclusion must be qualified in some respects: not all of the rise and fall in the value of grain held in commercial channels will be reflected in farm income. During years when futures trading has been in operation at least part of the rise or fall in the value of grain accrues to the holder of futures contracts. The speculator, the normal holder of these futures, might not treat his gains or losses in the same way as he would ordinary income. Thus, the effects of these gains and losses on spending is uncertain. Further, in the period before 1930, part of the rise or fall in the value of grain accrued to the Canadian Co-operative Wheat Producers (the Pools) and was reflected in payments to the farmers only after a lag. Similarly during recent years all of the wheat in commercial channels and most of the coarse grains have been held by the Canadian Wheat Board. In these circumstances the rise or fall in the value of grain held at the end of the year is reflected mainly in the profits of the Board and these may not be distributed for a year or more. During the 1930's a substantial quantity of wheat and grain options were held on behalf of the Dominion government by an organization known as the Central Selling Agency.[8] During this period a substantial proportion of the rise and fall in the book value of grain was reflected in the accounts of this organization. The Agency's gains and losses had no immediate effect on spending.

Though the difference between the change in quantity and the change in value of grain in commercial channels is usually not large, in some years it is extremely important. For six years during the period 1926 to 1950 the difference exceeded $85 million and in one year, 1930, the difference amounted to more than $200 million.

In relation to national income the value of grain in commercial channels has fluctuated irregularly. A comparison of the annual change in the value of investment in grain with the corresponding annual change in the value of gross national product shows that the value of investment in grain moved in the opposite direction to the value of gross national product in fourteen out of the twenty-four comparisons. This irregularity is due both to variations in crop yield and to price fluctuations. When one of these opposite movements precedes a turning point in the business cycle it may be a contributory factor in causing the turning point. Thus the rise in the value of investment in grain from 1932 to 1933 amounted to about 20 per cent of the decline in gross national product between these two years. This may have assisted the revival that occurred in May 1933. Again, in the 1937-8 decline the increase in the value of investment in grain amounted to about 60 per cent of the decline in value of gross national product and this may have been an important factor in moderating the fall in income at that time. But there are numerous instances where an equally large change in the value of annual investment in grain had no perceptible effect on the course of the cycle. Thus the increase in investment in grain from 1930 to 1931 amounted to about 30 per cent of the decline in gross national product but income and employment continued to fall at about the same rate.

The volume of grain held in Canada has fluctuated from year to year with variations in the size of crop. Over the period 1929 to 1937 it moved in a roughly counter-cyclical fashion, a pattern similar to that followed by world stocks of primary commodities. In Canada the price stabilization policy followed by the Dominion government played an important part in financing the accumulation of surplus stocks.[9]

Substantial quantities of grain may be held on the farm as well as in commercial storage. In the main, grain held on the farm at the end of any year will represent unrealized income, a part of the return to the farmer's own labour and investment for that year. As such, it is unlikely to affect spending appreciably in the year in which it accrues. Farmers may anticipate the income that will be received when the grain is subsequently sold but their ability to do so will be limited by their access to credit and their willingness to go into debt for this purpose. Where this does occur it seems probable that here, too, the change in market value of grain will be more significant than the change in quantity.[10]

Economists have often suggested that business firms will accumulate stocks when prices are rising and are expected to rise further and will liquidate their stocks when they anticipate falling prices. To be completely successful, speculative activity of this type would require business firms to accumulate stocks when prices are low and liquidate them before the peak. There is little evidence that such a policy is followed; for manufacturing inventories almost the reverse seems to be true. Some of the most rapid accumulations of manufacturer's stocks occur in the year following a downturn, usually a period of falling prices; substantial reductions in stocks often occur during the year following an upturn, usually a period of rising prices.

Moreover, data on the ratio of inventories to total output show that business firms usually reduce their inventories by less than the decline in their sales during periods of contraction and increase them by less than the rise in their sales during periods of expansion. Over the cycle as a whole the ratio of stocks to output usually moves in a counter-cyclical fashion. This is evident in Table 26 which shows the ratio of total inventories to gross national product over the

TABLE 26

Ratio of Total Inventories to Gross National Product, 1935-9 Prices, Canada, 1926 to 1950 °

		Per cent			
1926	44	1934	54	1942	36
1927	44	1935	51	1943	35
1928	44	1936	48	1944	32
1929	46	1937	43	1945	32
1930	49	1938	44	1946	33
1931	57	1939	45	1947	35
1932	59	1940	44	1948	36
1933	62	1941	41	1949	36
				1950	36

° Ratio of average beginning and year-end inventory in $ 1935-1939 to annual gross national product in $ 1935-1939.

SOURCE: *National Accounts: Income and Expenditure, 1926 to 1950* (Ottawa, 1952).

TABLE 27

Ratio of Inventory to Gross Value of Production, Manufacturing, Canada, 1919 to 1948 °

		Per cent			
1919	23.9	1929	21.8	1939	21.9
1920	22.4	1930	26.0	1940	19.6
1921	32.0	1931	30.3	1941	18.9
1922	27.8	1932	33.0	1942	18.6
1923	23.7	1933	29.8	1943	19.5
1924	25.3	1934	24.5	1944	21.1
1925	24.0	1935	22.8	1945	21.1
1926	22.4	1936	21.1	1946	19.5
1927	22.4	1937	19.4	1947	18.4
1928	22.1	1938	22.4	1948	18.9

° Ratio of the average beginning and year-end inventory to the annual gross value of production.

SOURCE: *The Manufacturing Industries of Canada, Annual Reports* (Ottawa, 1930-5, 1940-4).

period 1926 to 1950. A similar counter-cyclical pattern appears in the ratio of manufacturer's stocks to the gross value of manufacturing output. This ratio is shown in Table 27. The period of rapidly rising prices, 1919-20, has often been cited as an instance in which a speculative accumulation of inventories accentuated the rise in prices. There is no evidence to suggest that this was true of manufacturing inventories. The ratio of stocks to gross value of output in manufacturing was comparatively low in both 1919 and 1920. It was only after sales had fallen sharply in 1921 that this ratio increased.

Some conclusions may now be drawn. Investment in inventories though of little importance as a long-run source of demand has accounted for about 9 per cent of the cyclical variation in income in Canada. In this respect it is only about one-third as important as in the United States. This can be explained by the less frequent occurrence of minor recessions in Canada, by the greater willingness of Canadian business firms to allow a rise in their stock-sales ratio during periods of depression and by the greater tendency of Canadian investment in inventories to lead or lag at cyclical turning points.

In general, investment in inventories in Canada has reinforced expansions and contractions in the level of income and at times has contributed to revivals or recessions in business. But it exerts a somewhat irregular influence on the economy: in some years a rise in investment in inventories has accounted for the major part of an increase in total spending; in others it has moved in the opposite direction to income and employment. If other expenditure forces are sufficiently strong, a decline in investment in inventories will have no adverse effects on general prosperity. This irregularity is also present in the timing of investment in inventories at cyclical turning points. Though investment in non-agricultural inventories often reaches its peak and trough in the same year as business activity as a whole, leads and lags also occur. Fluctuations in the value of investment in inventories also appear to exert an important causal influence on the economy. Changes in the value of total inventory parallel changes in the value of commercial bank loans and this suggests that fluctuations in the value of inventories may play an important role in inflationary and deflationary periods.

Manufacturing inventories have shown a long lag at cyclical turning points. Between 1919 and 1937 their average lag behind the monthly turning points in the business cycle was fifteen months. This long lag often resulted in a peak in investment in manufacturing inventories in the year following a reference peak. While peaks in investment were typically reached in the year of the reference peak or the year following, a trough in investment was often reached in the year immediately following a peak. This series showed no consistent relation to the minor cycle. In the period 1931 to 1934 Canadian manufacturers carried abnormally large stocks of raw materials and finished goods in relation to their level of output. In addition, an unusually large proportion of their inventory was held in the form of finished goods. Both of these facts support the view of Hawtrey that in periods of subnormal activity increased output can begin at all stages of production more or less simultaneously. Keynes has argued that increased supplies of a product will be available only after a complete period of production has elapsed.

Somewhat diverse patterns of behaviour appear in the inventory held by the other major sectors of the economy. In the wholesale and retail field there is little evidence in annual data of any lag in the volume of inventory at cyclical turning points. Logging inventories move promptly at cyclical turning points. On the other hand inventories in the public utility field show an exceptionally long lag. Neither railway nor mining inventories have shown a regular cyclical pattern and the size of the annual crop imparts unpredictable variations into grain inventories. The varied behaviour of inventories in these different sectors will be reflected in the movement of total inventories.

The popular belief that speculative motives are an important determinant of inventory movements receives little support from Canadian data. Some of the most rapid increases in manufacturing inventories have occurred during periods when it would have been to the advantage of speculators to reduce their stocks. Furthermore, in both manufacturers' stocks and inventories in the economy as a whole, there is a marked tendency for the ratio of stocks to output to move in a counter-cyclical fashion.

CHAPTER TWELVE

CONCLUSION

THIS STATISTICAL STUDY of the behaviour of inventories in the Canadian economy confirms some theoretical views about intentories and contradicts others. The present analysis of annual data gives some support to the view that the movement of inventories may play a causal role at cyclical turning points, yet a more decisive statement must await the accumulation of monthly data. On the other hand, Canadian data give only limited support to the view that investment in inventories is an important cause of the minor recession. Canadian experience also suggests that the effects of investment in inventories in reinforcing cyclical expansions and contractions in income are much more irregular than any theoretical argument might lead one to expect. Investment in inventories may exert an important influence in one direction in one year only to be followed by an opposite movement in the following year. Though variations in agricultural output are responsible for much of this irregularity, industrial inventories as well show irregular variations. In addition, Canadian data heavily emphasize the fact that a decline or increase in the rate of investment in inventories does not automatically cause a similar change in economic activity. As often as not these changes may be offset by opposite changes in other expenditure forces.

Theoretical discussions of inventories have generally stressed the effects of changes in the volume of inventories as opposed to the effects of changes in the value of inventories. This study indicates that the changes in value deserve more attention. These changes may often be large, particularly in inventories of grain, and there is some evidence that they may be a neglected factor in analyses of the causes of inflation and deflation.

The varying patterns of inventory behaviour in different sectors of the economy underline the need for the study of the various components of total inventories. Yet a knowledge of the diverse movements that occur in individual types of inventory is not sufficient to explain the behaviour of inventories as a whole. The key to an understanding of the latter lies in an analysis of the relation of inventory movements to the equilibrium level of income. Such an analysis is essential in explaining what conditions must be met before the economy as a whole can achieve a planned accumulation or reduction in inventories.

STATISTICAL APPENDIX

TABLE I

THE PULP AND PAPER INDUSTRY, CANADA, 1918 TO 1950

Year	Value of inventory year-end ($ million)	Price index, pulpwood used (1937 = 100)	Pulpwood used in manufacture (million cords)	Value of inventory, $ 1937(a) ($ million)	Stock-production ratio(b)	Invest-ment in inventories, $ 1937
1918	39.7	140	2.2	25.1	1.50	
1919	46.6	158	2.4	23.3	1.26	— 1.8
1920	66.2	200	2.8	31.1	1.47	7.8
1921	74.6	213	2.2	43.9	2.65	—12.8
1922	55.9	170	2.9	34.6	1.56	— 9.3
1923	60.3	161	3.3	36.9	1.48	2.3
1924	68.1	164	3.3	42.4	1.68	5.5
1925	60.0	161	3.7	37.7	1.35	— 4.7
1926	63.4	159	4.2	40.7	1.26	3.0
1927	69.8	156	4.4	44.8	1.34	4.1
1928	86.0	156	4.8	56.1	1.55	11.3
1929	66.7	153	5.2	44.8	1.13	—11.3
1930	83.1	149	4.6	63.1	1.79	18.3
1931	57.7	132	4.1	50.4	1.63	—12.7
1932	42.5	115	3.6	46.2	1.69	— 4.2
1933	33.7	92	4.0	38.7	1.34	— 7.5
1934	37.8	87	4.8	42.5	1.18	3.8
1935	41.6	89	5.0	45.5	1.20	3.0
1936	41.4	91	5.8	41.4	.94	— 4.1
1937	52.3	100	6.6	47.6	.95	6.2
1938	60.5	110	4.7	54.4	1.53	6.8
1939	56.6	111	5.4	49.2	1.21	— 5.2
1940	74.4	115	6.9	61.2	1.16	12.0
1941	78.5	122	7.7	55.6	.95	— 5.6
1942	86.8	141	7.7	52.4	.90	— 3.2
1943	83.0	166	7.3	44.0	.80	— 8.4
1944	74.7	189	7.2	35.5	.65	— 8.5
1945	82.3	210	7.5	36.0	.63	.5
1946	105.6	229	8.7	38.8	.59	2.8
1947	143.7	272	9.5	48.1	.66	9.3
1948	177.6	300	10.2	59.1	.76	11.0
1949	165.3	300	10.2	56.5	.73	— 2.6
1950	158.3	293	11.1	47.0	.56	— 9.5

(a) Deflated by price of pulpwood used for manufacture in the following year.

(b) Ratio of year-end inventory valued at 1937 prices to pulpwood consumed in the current year valued at $7.60 per cord.

SOURCE: Canada, D.B.S., Annual Reports, *The Pulp and Paper Industry.*

TABLE II

THE NON-FERROUS SMELTING AND REFINING INDUSTRY, CANADA, 1918 TO 1950

Year	Value of inventory year-end ($ million)	Price index, non-ferrous metals (1935-9 = 100)	Gross value of production $ 1935-9(a) ($ million)	Value of inventory, 1935-9(b) ($ million)	Stock-production ratio(c)	Investment in inventories, $ 1935-9 ($ million)
1918	18.6	193	32	9.6		
1919	19.1	182	28	10.0	35	.4
1920	25.8	184	n.a.	17.1	n.a.	7.1
1921	21.8	132	18	16.6	93	— .5
1922	11.1	132	18	8.3	69	— 8.3
1923	12.1	130	27	9.5	33	1.2
1924	13.9	129	33	10.6	30	1.1
1925	12.7	141	40	8.9	24	— 1.7
1926	17.0	136	54	13.2	20	4.3
1927	19.2	124	63	15.6	23	2.4
1928	22.5	125	75	17.8	22	2.2
1929	21.9	135	81	16.7	21	— 1.1
1930	29.4	110	92	30.1	25	13.4
1931	29.4	88	112	34.3	29	4.2
1932	28.3	80	96	36.1	37	1.8
1933	29.2	87	116	31.9	34	— 4.2
1934	30.8	87	172	35.9	20	4.0
1935	27.2	94	198	28.0	16	— 7.9
1936	24.2	95	242	24.8	11	— 3.2
1937	29.0	115	277	29.0	10	4.2
1938	34.7	97	296	35.6	11	6.6
1939	35.1	98	268	35.2	13	— .4
1940	42.5	105	291	40.3	13	5.1
1941	49.4	106	358	46.8	12	6.5
1942	66.7	107	418	62.0	13	15.2
1943	83.7	109	468	78.0	15	16.0
1944	42.3	109	435	39.0	13	—39.0
1945	38.1	109	326	35.0	11	— 4.0
1946	35.5	121	252	29.1	13	— 5.9
1947	56.9	170	266	31.3	11	2.2
1948	76.4	204	282	35.4	12	4.1
1949	77.9	198	302	41.6	13	6.2
1950	83.0	221	303	37.8	13	— 3.8

(a) Deflated by annual price index of non-ferrous metals (excluding gold).

(b) Deflated by index of non-ferrous metal prices (excluding gold) for the last six months of the year or December if lower.

(c) Ratio of average beginning and year-end inventory in $1935-9 dollars to gross value of production in $1935-9.

SOURCE: D.B.S., Annual Reports, *The Non-Ferrous Smelting and Refining Industry.*

TABLE III

THE LUMBER INDUSTRY, CANADA, 1918 TO 1950

Year	Value of inventory year-end ($ million)	Porduction sawn lumber billion ft.B.M.	Value of inventory, $ 1935-9(a) ($ million)	Price index lumber (1935-9 = 100)	Stock-production ratio(b)	Invest-ment in inventories, $ 1935-9 ($ million)
1918	55.1	3.9	48.0	115	49	
1919	66.8	3.8	47.8	140	50	— .2
1920	68.2	4.3	45.6	158	43	— 2.2
1921	69.5	2.9	55.8	141	70	10.2
1922	51.3	3.1	45.2	117	65	—10.6
1923	48.7	3.7	41.2	122	47	— 4.0
1924	58.2	3.9	54.2	117	49	13.0
1925	63.6	3.9	58.0	112	57	3.8
1926	60.5	4.2	57.5	112	55	— .5
1927	58.0	4.1	54.0	109	54	— 3.5
1928	59.4	4.3	51.3	115	49	— 2.7
1929	60.5	4.7	53.5	118	45	2.2
1930	59.0	4.0	65.5	100	60	12.0
1931	41.6	2.5	54.6	84	96	—10.9
1932	21.8	1.8	31.2	75	95	—23.4
1933	18.0	2.0	23.7	78	55	— 7.5
1934	17.0	2.6	21.2	87	35	— 2.5
1935	19.8	3.0	24.1	86	30	2.9
1936	20.8	3.4	23.1	97	28	— 1.0
1937	27.8	4.0	28.5	110	26	5.4
1938	30.2	3.8	32.1	99	32	3.6
1939	27.6	4.0	27.4	106	30	— 4,7
1940	28.7	4.6	25.9	118	23	— 1.5
1941	30.1	4.9	22.9	137	20	— 3.0
1942	30.0	4.9	21.2	153	18	— 1.7
1943	29.8	4.4	18.6	170	16	— 2.6
1944	49.7	4.5	29.2	184	21	10.6
1945	51.4	4.5	27.8	185	25	— 1.4
1946	55.8	5.1	27.5	198	22	— .3
1947	73.4	5.9	26.4	263	18	— 1.1
1948	91.7	5.6	27.3	330	19	.9
1949	76.3	5.4	22.2	349	18	— 5.1
1950	83.8	5.9	20.6	388	15	— 1.6

(a) Deflated by price index of lumber for 8 months ending in December, or December, if lower, adjusted to remove sales tax.

(b) Ratio of average beginning and year-end inventory in 1937 prices to annual production of sawn lumber valued at $25.00 per M. bd. ft.

SOURCE: D.B.S., Annual Reports, *The Lumber Industry.*

TABLE IV

THE TOBACCO INDUSTRIES, CANADA, 1918 TO 1950

Year	Value of inventory year-end ($ million)	Farm price raw tobacco (¢ per lb.)	Commercial leaf crop (million lbs.)	Tobacco taken for manufacture (million lbs.)	Value of inventory, $ 1937(a) ($ million)	Invest-ment in inventories, $ 1937 ($ million)
1918	19.2	35	12.4	n.a.	11.0	
1919	20.5	46	29.4	31.2	11.3	.3
1920	29.4	12	41.8	26.7	19.3	8.0
1921	24.1	18	11.5	28.0	22.5	3.2
1922	21.9	17	22.6	36.1	19.2	— 3.3
1923	20.7	16	18.5	30.5	18.0	— 1.2
1924	20.2	23	16.3	31.8	13.6	— 4.4
1925	18.9	24	25.4	31.7	15.3	1.7
1926	18.6	26	25.1	36.6	14.2	— 1.1
1927	19.8	20	38.2	37.2	16.0	1.8
1928	22.2	16	36.5	39.6	19.8	3.8
1929	25.2	20	25.9	43.2	20.0	.2
1930	29.2	19	31.7	37.6	23.3	3.3
1931	27.4	14	44.4	34.0	25.4	2.1
1932	24.8	11	46.8	33.8	25.1	— .3
1933	23.6	14	39.0	34.7	24.4	— .7
1934	22.5	19	33.6	36.1	23.3	— 1.1
1935	25.9	20	48.2	38.8	26.9	3.6
1936	25.0	20	40.0	39.1	25.0	— 1.9
1937	25.2	24	62.8	43.6	26.0	1.0
1938	28.2	20	88.3	43.8	31.2	5.2
1939	26.6	18	93.7	46.7	31.8	.6
1940	35.6	17	55.7	50.9	43.7	11.9
1941	35.3	20	81.9	54.6	44.2	.5
1942	43.3	24	78.0	63.4	50.8	6.6
1943	48.6	28	60.0	68.4	50.0	— .8
1944	52.3	29	91.7	71.7	48.5	— 1.5
1945	57.4	33	80.3	77.1	46.4	— 2.1
1946	57.1	35	122.9	73.1	44.6	— 1.8
1947	64.9	35	92.8	75.5	48.0	3.4
1948	80.1	40	110.1	77.2	55.0	7.0
1949	88.7	40	121.6	80.3	60.0b	5.0
1950	97.3	43	104.6	78.2	65.0b	5.0

(a) Deflated by average price of tobacco used for manufacture in the following year.

SOURCE: D.B.S., Annual Reports, *The Tobacco Industries.*

TABLE V

THE PETROLEUM PRODUCTS INDUSTRY, CANADA, 1918 TO 1950

Year	Value of inventory year-end ($ million)	Price index petroleum products (1935-9 = 100)	Gross value production $ 1935-9(a) ($ million)	Value of inventory, 1935-9(b) ($ million)	Stock-production ratio(c)	Invest-ment in inventories, $ 1935-9 ($ million)
1918	12.1	151	25	8.0		
1919	13.1	156	28	8.4	.29	.4
1920	17.3	192	30	9.0	.29	.6
1921	18.0	170	30	11.6	.34	2.6
1922	19.4	158	36	12.3	.33	.7
1923	12.3	131	35	9.4	.31	— 2.9
1924	18.3	134	37	13.6	.31	4.2
1925	19.0	126	40	15.1	.36	1.5
1926	21.3	138	52	15.4	.29	.3
1927	19.0	124	52	15.3	.29	— .1
1928	19.4	118	70	16.4	.23	1.1
1929	30.6	119	84	25.8	.25	9.4
1930	24.0	116	79	21.6	.30	— 4.2
1931	21.7	101	76	21.5	.29	— .1
1932	22.7	103	70	22.0	.31	.5
1933	21.1	103	68	20.5	.31	— 1.5
1934	22.0	105	72	21.0	.29	.5
1935	25.2	102	79	24.7	.29	3.7
1936	24.9	99	87	25.2	.29	.5
1937	27.9	102	96	27.4	.27	2.2
1938	27.0	100	96	27.0	.28	— .4
1939	29.3	96	108	30.5	.27	3.5
1940	37.4	107	114	35.0	.29	4.5
1941	40.0	115	136	34.8	.26	— .2
1942	40.2	120	136	33.4	.25	— 1.4
1943	41.5	121	155	34.3	.22	.9
1944	46.3	120	175	38.6	.21	4.3
1945	47.3	117	172	40.4	.23	1.8
1946	52.3	117	190	44.7	.22	4.3
1947	69.3	126	228	55.0	.22	10.3
1948	100.0	155	255	64.5	.23	9.5
1949	93.6	160	273	59.2	.23	— 5.3
1950	106.4	168	306	63.5		4.3

(a) Deflated by annual price index of petroleum product.

(b) Deflated by price index of petroleum products for the last six months of year.

(c) Ratio of average beginning and year-end inventory in $1935-9 to production in $1935-9.

SOURCE: D.B.S., Annual Reports, *The Petroleum Products Industry.*

TABLE VI

THE ELECTRICAL APPARATUS AND SUPPLIES INDUSTRY, CANADA, 1918 TO 1950

Year	Value of inventory ($ million)	Gross value of production ($ million) Value of	$ 1935-9(a) inventory, 1935-9(b) ($ million)	Stock-production ratio(c)	Invest-ment in inventories, $ 1935-9 ($ million)
1918	17.1	16	9.3		
1919	15.0	22	8.9	41	— .4
1920	24.3	31	14.8	39	5.9
1921	18.4	34	15.0	44	.2
1922	17.4	36	14.0	40	— 1.0
1923	18.8	42	15.0	35	1.0
1924	19.8	47	16.1	33	1.1
1925	19.4	51	15.3	30	.8
1926	20.7	62	17.1	26	1.8
1927	20.5	74	18.2	24	1.1
1928	21.5	90	19.0	21	.8
1929	24.3	106	20.8	19	1.8
1930	23.3	106	24.4	21	3.6
1931	20.4	91	23.0	26	— 1.4
1932	17.6	61	20.9	36	— 2.1
1933	16.5	42	18.1	46	— 2.8
1934	17.0	56	19.2	33	1.1
1935	16.9	67	17.8	28	1.4
1936	20.4	77	21.7	26	3.9
1937	29.8	90	28.7	28	7.0
1938	25.4	88	25.4	31	— 3.3
1939	28.6	87	28.0	30	2.6
1940	40.4	121	37.4	27	9.4
1941	51.0	162	45.6	26	8.2
1942	58.1	187	51.0	26	5.4
1943	69.6	218	61.0	26	10.0
1944	65.5	250	56.8	24	4.2
1945	69.7	204	60.3	29	3.5
1946	80.2	195	62.5	31	2.2
1947	111.7	250	68.0	26	5.5
1948	115.4	248	59.0	26	— 9.0
1949	102.7	274	53.8	21	— 5.2
1950	137.0	304	61.7	19	7.9

(a) Deflated by annual index of iron and steel and non-ferrous metal prices (excluding gold).

(b) Deflated by a price index of iron and steel products (weight, 40 %) and non-ferrous metals ex. gold (weight, 60 %) for 6 months ending in Dec. or Dec. if lower.

(c) Ratio of average beginning and year-end inventory in $1935-9 to annual gross value of production in $1935-9.

SOURCE: D.B.S., Annual Reports, *The Electrical Apparatus and Supplies Industry.*

TABLE VII

THE PRIMARY IRON AND STEEL INDUSTRY, CANADA, 1918 TO 1950

Year	Value of inventory year-end ($ million)	Gross value of production $ 1935-9(a) ($ million)	Value of inventory, 1935-9(b) ($ million)	Stock-production ratio(c)	Price index, Iron and its products (1935-9 = 100)	Invest-ment in inventories, $ 1935-9 ($ million)
1918	28.1	149	17.2		164	
1919	22.6	78	16.0	21	146	— 1.2
1920	28.1	79	15.6	20	176	— .6
1921	19.5	42	17.7	40	134	2.1
1922	12.7	32	11.2	45	110	— 6.5
1923	14.2	54	11.6	21	121	.4
1924	11.1	29	9.8	37	116	— 1.8
1925	9.0	32	8.4	28	110	— 1.4
1926	10.0	39	9.6	23	105	1.2
1927	12.9	45	12.9	25	101	3.3
1928	15.3	64	15.7	22	98	2.8
1929	17.2	74	17.5	22	98	1.8
1930	22.2	55	23.4	37	96	5.9
1931	18.0	40	19.7	54	92	— 3.7
1932	14.1	18	15.5	98	90	— 4.2
1933	13.5	21	14.9	72	89	— .6
1934	14.0	32	15.3	47	91	.4
1935	16.1	42	17.5	39	92	2.2
1936	16.9	50	18.8	36	93	1.3
1937	21.4	71	19.5	27	105	.7
1938	23.8	56	23.1	38	106	3.6
1939	22.8	72	21.7	31	105	— 1.4
1940	30.3	105	27.3	23	109	5.6
1941	40.8	146	34.4	21	113	7.1
1942	45.4	200	37.3	18	116	2.9
1943	48.0	192	39.4	20	117	2.1
1944	47.9	180	39.0	22	118	— .4
1945	46.1	163	37.4	23	118	— 1.6
1946	35.4	120	26.1	26	127	—11.3
1947	52.8	154	36.5	20	141	10.4
1948	68.7	175	39.6	22	161	3.1
1949	66.2	174	36.2	22	175	— 3.4
1950	67.3	183	34.4	19	184	— 1.8

(a) Deflated by annual price index of iron and its products.

(b) Deflated by price index of iron and its products for 6 months ending in Dec. or Dec. if lower.

(c) Ratio of average beginning and year-end inventory in $1935-9 to deflated gross value of production.

SOURCE: D.B.S., Annual Reports, *The Primary Iron and Steel Industry.*

TABLE VIII

THE AGRICULTURAL IMPLEMENTS INDUSTRY, CANADA, 1918 TO 1950

Year	Value of inventory year-end ($ million)	Price index, farm machinery to the farmer (1935-9 = 100)	Gross value of production, $ 1935-9(a) ($ million)	Value of inventory, 1935-9(b) ($ million)	Stock-production ratio(c)	Investment in inventories, $ 1935-9 ($ million)
1918	29.6	82	47	18		
1919	34.9	87	47	24	45	5.9
1920	42.4	92	55	24	44	.1
1921	36.0	111	35	33	81	8.8
1922	29.3	90	20	27	150	— 6.1
1923	31.0	93	28	26	95	— 1.2
1924	29.6	102	26	25	98	— .1
1925	28.0	98	25	26	102	.1
1926	29.0	98	39	28	69	2.1
1927	32.1	98	44	32	68	4.2
1928	34.1	98	42	35	78	3.1
1929	39.9	98	42	41	90	5.7
1930	31.3	97	28	33	132	— 7.2
1931	28.0	95	12	31	267	— 2.8
1932	20.1	94	6	22	442	— 8.4
1933	19.2	92	6	21	358	— .8
1934	14.8	95	9	16	206	— 5.2
1935	15.7	95	14	17	118	.9
1936	17.2	98	16	19	112	1.5
1937	21.6	97	20	20	97	1.9
1938	21.0	104	20	20	100	— .2
1939	18.0	104	15	17	123	— 3.1
1940	18.7	106	21	17	81	—
1941	21.5	109	32	19	51	1.9
1942	20.5	114	39	18	47	— 1.4
1943	23.0	117	49	20	39	2.0
1944	24.0	119	51	20	39	.7
1945	24.9	115	50	21	41	.7
1946	36.0	119	53	28	46	7.2
1947	48.1	125	71	34	44	5.8
1948	55.7	143	103	34	33	.4
1949	47.8	158	112	27	27	— 7.2
1950	48.5	165	91	26	29	— .9

(a) Deflated by price index of farm machinery to farmer adjusted to remove sales tax.

(b) Deflated by annual price index of iron and its products or Dec. if lower.

(c) Ratio of beginning and year-end inventory in $1935-9 to deflated gross value of production.

SOURCE: D.B.S., Annual Reports, *The Agricultural Implements Industry*.

TABLE IX

THE FRUIT AND VEGETABLE PREPARATIONS INDUSTRY, CANADA, 1918 TO 1950

Year	Value of inventory year-end ($ million)	Price index, canned fruit and vegetables (1935-9 = 100)	Value of inventory, $ 1935-9(a) ($ million)	Gross value of production, 1935-9(b) ($ million)	Stock-sales ratio(c)	Invest-ment in inventories, $ 1935-9 ($ million)
1918	7.3	193	3.8	14.1	.27	
1919	7.6	194	3.9	16.0	.24	.1
1920	12.8	196	6.5	17.8	.35	2.6
1921	9.4	166	5.7	12.6	.45	— .8
1922	9.6	165	5.8	14.3	.41	.1
1923	7.0	152	4.6	13.7	.34	— 1.2
1924	9.2	167	5.5	16.1	.34	.9
1925	11.9	172	7.3	17.6	.41	1.8
1926	14.4	141	10.2	21.4	.48	2.9
1927	14.8	140	10.5	21.6	.49	.3
1928	15.3	139	11.0	25.4	.43	.5
1929	15.7	141	11.1	28.4	.39	.1
1930	21.1	137	17.4	31.5	.55	6.3
1931	17.8	104	20.4	31.5	.65	3.0
1932	15.5	99	15.7	30.2	.52	— 4.7
1933	13.3	103	12.9	29.1	.44	— 2.8
1934	13.9	100	13.8	35.2	.39	.9
1935	13.1	99	13.3	38.8	.34	— .5
1936	14.4	100	14.4	47.2	.31	1.1
1937	18.2	109	16.7	46.2	.36	2.3
1938	19.6	98	20.0	48.7	.41	3.3
1939	16.0	97	16.6	57.2	.29	— 3.4
1940	15.8	108	14.7	51.3	.29	— 1.9
1941	20.2	112	18.0	67.6	.27	3.3
1942	18.2	110	16.6	67.0	.25	— 1.4
1943	24.1	109	22.1	66.1	.33	5.5
1944	26.1	110	23.8	97.8	.24	1.7
1945	25.6	110	23.2	90.3	.26	— .6
1946	34.9	121	28.8	112.2	.26	5.6
1947	43.2	143	29.9	106.6	.28	1.1
1948	52.0	159	32.6	103.9	.31	2.7
1949	69.9	155	47.8	96.0	.50	15.2
1950	66.0	145	45.5	111.2	.42	— 2.3

(a) Deflated by annual price index of canned fruits and vegetables, adjusted to lower of cost or market.

(b) Deflated by annual index of canned fruits and vegetables.

(c) Ratio of stocks at year-end in $1935-9 to the current year's gross value of production in $1935-9.

SOURCE: D.B.S., Annual Reports, *Fruit and Vegetable Preparations Industry*.

TABLE X

THE DISTILLED LIQUOR INDUSTRY, CANADA, 1918 TO 1950

Year	Value of inventory year-end ($ million)	Spirits in Warehouse	Spirits manufactured	Liquor released or exported(a)	Stock-sales ratio(b)	Investment in inventories, Spirits in warehouse)
		Fiscal years ended March 31 (million proof gallons)				
1918	4.0	13.0	3.6	5.4	2.4	
1919	1.0	10.7	4.2	3.4	3.2	— 2.3
1920	3.0	6.9	2.4	5.4	1.3	— 3.8
1921	3.5	6.2	4.2	3.9	1.6	— .7
1922	4.4	8.2	5.0	.9	9.1	2.0
1923	4.8	8.7	3.8	1.0	8.7	.5
1924	7.4	8.7	4.4	1.8	4.8	—
1925	9.7	11.7	7.3	1.7	6.9	3.0
1926	12.3	12.8	5.4	1.6	8.0	1.1
1927	19.4	16.4	9.1	2.0	8.2	3.6
1928	25.3	21.8	11.6	2.5	8.7	5.4
1929	32.8	30.8	16.8	3.1	9.9	9.0
1930	34.9	39.9	16.8	3.7	10.8	9.1
1931	33.4	41.9	9.3	3.8	11.0	2.0
1932	32.2	42.5	7.1	3.1	13.7	.6
1933	31.8	40.8	4.3	2.8	14.6	— 1.7
1934	28.4	40.1	6.4	3.4	11.8	— .7
1935	25.8	37.0	4.3	3.3	11.2	— 3.1
1936	21.6	34.2	6.6	4.6	7.4	— 2.8
1937	19.7	30.1	8.7	7.2	4.2	— 4.1
1938	17.5	28.2	10.2	6.9	4.1	— 1.9
1939	17.9	28.7	9.6	4.3	6.7	.5
1940	20.2	32.5	11.8	3.9	8.3	3.8
1941	20.5	36.0	14.6	5.7	6.3	3.5
1942	23.5	38.7	17.6	5.0	7.7	2.7
1943	23.2	40.8	19.7	6.8	6.0	2.1
1944	25.6	36.4	27.2	20.0	1.8	— 4.4
1945	30.4	42.6	35.6	18.6	2.3	6.2
1946	41.4	52.7	34.6	16.0	3.3	10.1
1947	57.4	56.0	21.6	9.2	6.1	3.5
1948	71.9	67.1	28.2	8.5	7.9	11.1
1949	73.6	72.8	23.6	8.5	8.6	5.7
1950	80.8	78.2	20.7	8.5	9.2	5.4

(a) Matured liquors released for consumption or exported in bond.

(b) Ratio of year-end stocks of spirits to matured liquors released for consumption or exported in bond during the preceding year.

SOURCE: D.B.S., Annual Reports, *The Control and Sale of Alcoholic Beverages in Canada,* and *The Distilled Liquor Industry.*

TABLE XI

VALUE OF INVESTMENT IN INVENTORIES, BY INDUSTRY, CANADA, 1926 TO 1950

Year	Farm	Logging	Mining	Manufacturing	Construction	Transportation Communication
			Million dollars			
1926	— 1	— 1	—	27	8	— 6
1927	60	5	2	48	2	3
1928	— 22	—	1	72	4	1
1929	—129	4	4	42	11	9
1930	46	—12	— 2	— 30	—14	— 6
1931	— 30	— 7	1	—129	—13	— 9
1932	14	— 3	— 4	—112	—16	— 5
1933	— 33	6	3	— 24	1	—13
1934	— 8	7	2	24	4	— 4
1935	— 1	1	—	13	2	4
1936	— 56	8	9	41	— 1	— 1
1937	— 11	17	1	107	8	5
1938	28	—25	2	— 18	— 3	— 3
1939	60	9	3	46	1	3
1940	75	12	3	140	7	5
1941	— 48	1	10	166	12	19
1942	354	2	3	— 26	—11	10
1943	—125	4	— 4	153	— 4	7
1944	—103	13	— 1	43	—12	10
1945	—231	32	— 2	123	6	—11
1946	— 57	58	14	244	5	10
1947	— 79	— 4	10	515	19	22
1948	— 65	4	2	267	18	36
1949	— 72	—34	4	104	33	—15
1950	131	26	2	404	15	9

Data for farm inventories are value of physical change. All other data are change in book value.

Source: D.B.S., *National Accounts: Income and Expenditure, 1926-1950* (Ottawa, 1952).

TABLE XI

(continued)

Year	Public utility	Grain in storage	Wholesale	Retail	Total current value	Total $ 1935-9
			Million dollars			
1926	— 1	— 44	35	47	65	119
1927	4	40	19	47	231	216
1928	— 8	60	— 13	63	160	158
1929	—	50	13	71	77	48
1930	—	—220	— 26	— 62	—326	126
1931	—	2	— 52	— 27	—266	—159
1932	—	— 23	— 33	— 62	—246	— 80
1933	— 1	55	— 20	— 10	— 37	—125
1934	—	59	20	4	109	23
1935	—	1	13	13	47	48
1936	—	— 39	26	20	8	—113
1937	1	— 89	26	31	98	35
1938	1	17	— 25	— 9	— 36	127
1939	1	188	45	35	392	338
1940	1	52	15	20	331	316
1941	2	14	40	31	250	53
1942	—	90	— 3	— 25	396	214
1943	— 2	70	— 13	— 36	51	—120
1944	1	— 13	9	—	— 52	— 77
1945	3	—208	10	28	—248	—203
1946	7	— 38	125	146	522	226
1947	16	55	178	232	979	240
1948	22	47	140	130	601	85
1949	16	12	58	146	259	48
1950	— 1	8	166	178	948	386

TABLE XII

VALUE OF INVENTORY, FOUR INDUSTRIES, CANADA, 1918 TO 1925

Year	Railways	Manufacturing	Public utilities	Grain	Total

Million dollars

Value in current dollars as of December 31

Year	Railways	Manufacturing	Public utilities	Grain	Total
1918	40	782	5.9	469	1,297
1919	46	771	6.7	392	1,215
1920	75	904	9.6	398	1,387
1921	87	701	9.6	241	1,039
1922	76	630	10.1	298	1,014
1923	92	644	16.7	356	1,109
1924	85	672	18.2	424	1,199
1925	72	681	13.4	482	1,249

Value in $1935-9 as of December 31

Year	Railways	Manufacturing	Public utilities	Grain	Total
1918	44	487	6.1	226	763
1919	41	463	5.6	174	685
1920	53	486	6.2	255	799
1921	72	543	7.3	229	850
1922	66	493	8.2	269	836
1923	77	484	13.0	390	964
1924	75	517	15.1	248	856
1925	64	521	11.1	334	931

SOURCE: Data on railway inventories were obtained from D.B.S., Annual Reports, *The Transportation Industry*. Data for 1918 and 1919 were estimated on the assumption that total inventories moved in the same way as inventories of the C.P.R. and the Canadian Northern Railway. An index of the price of coal and lumber was used to deflate the current dollar values. Data on manufacturing and public utility inventories were obtained from D.B.S., Annual Reports, *The Manufacturing Industries of Canada*. Public utility inventories were deflated with the index used for railway inventories. Manufacturing inventories were deflated by wholesale price indexes corresponding to the nine main industrial groups. Data on grain and grain prices were obtained from the Canada Year Book.

TABLE XIII

INVESTMENT IN INVENTORIES, BY INDUSTRY, CANADA, 1926 TO 1950, AT CONSTANT PRICES

Year	Manufacturing	Other non-agricultural	Total non-agricultural	Grain in storage	Total all industries
		Million dollars			
1926	44	88	132	— 13	119
1927	55	91	146	28	216
1928	61	41	102	76	158
1929	42	90	132	5	48
1930	75	— 46	29	— 8	126
1931	— 49	— 15	— 64	— 38	—159
1932	— 54	— 89	—143	36	— 80
1933	— 53	— 26	— 79	8	—125
1934	3	17	20	15	23
1935	11	22	33	—	48
1936	20	51	71	—141	—113
1937	60	49	109	— 62	35
1938	20	4	— 24	108	127
1939	16	83	99	180	338
1940	78	4	82	140	316
1941	81	29	110	16	53
1942	— 66	— 53	—119	— 9	214
1943	105	— 61	44	— 91	—120
1944	20	— 7	13	— 6	— 77
1945	88	34	122	—188	—203
1946	91	204	295	— 38	226
1947	108	179	287	—	240
1948	—	55	55	32	85
1949	20	80	100	— 5	48
1950	115	138	253	58	386

All data are in 1935-9 dollars. Non-agricultural inventories exclude inventories on the farm and grain in commercial channels.

Source: Unpublished data, D.B.S.

NOTES

CHAPTER ONE

1. M. Abramovitz, *Inventories and Business Cycles* (New York, 1950), pp. 132-53.
2. M. Kalecki, *Essays in the Theory of Economic Fluctuations* (London, 1939), p. 120.
3. J. M. Clark, "Business Acceleration and the Law of Demand: A. Technical Factor in Economic Cycles," reprinted in *Readings in Business Cycle Theory* (Philadelphia, 1944), pp. 250-1.
4. See T. M. Whitin, *The Theory of Inventory Management* (Princeton, 1953).
5. *Ibid.*, p. 33.
6. Abramovitz, *Inventories and Business Cycles*, pp. 144-5.

CHAPTER TWO

1. A. H. Hansen, *Business Cycles and National Income* (New York, 1951), p. 19.
2. M. Abramovitz, *Inventories and Business Cycles* (New York, 1950), p. 497.
3. This view will be examined in more detail later. Its leading exponent is Professor L. A. Metzler. See his two articles, "The Nature and Stability of Inventory Cycles," *Review of Economic Statistics*, Aug., 1941, pp. 113-29 and "Factors Governing the Length of Inventory Cycles," *ibid.*, Feb., 1947, pp. 1-15.
4. J. M. Keynes, *The General Theory of Employment Interest and Money* (New York, 1936), p. 332.
5. The application of the acceleration principle to investment in inventories has been made by numerous writers. See, for example, G. Haberler, *Prosperity and Depression* (Geneva, 1941), pp. 94-5. Hansen appears to subscribe to all three interpretations. See *Business Cycles and National Income*, pp. 19-20, 184-7, and 471-6.
6. Abramovitz, *Inventories and Business Cycles*, p. 498.
7. Hansen, *Business Cycles and National Income*, p. 507.
8. See Hansen, *Fiscal Policy and Business Cycles* (New York, 1941), p. 54, and Abramovitz, *Inventories and Business Cycles*, p. 330.
9. A. G. Hart, *Money, Debt and Economic Activity* (New York, 1948), p. 303.
10. *Ibid.*, p. 324.
11. Abramovitz, *Inventories and Business Cycles*, pp. 127-31.
12. There is an extensive literature on this subject some of which will be noted later. One of the earliest references to come to my attention is the article by H. T. Warshow, "Inventory Valuation and the Business Cycle," *Harvard Business Review*, Oct., 1924.
13. J. M. Keynes, *Treatise on Money* (New York, 1930), II, pp. 102-47.
14. Keynes, *The General Theory of Employment Interest and Money*, pp. 313-32.
15. See the memorandum written in collaboration with R. B. Lewis, J. W. F. Rowe, and G. L. Schwartz, *Stocks of Staple Commodities* (London, 1923-30).
16. See R. G. Hawtrey, *Capital and Employment* (London, 1937), pp. 116-18.
17. Mr. Hawtrey's theories have been set forth in a number of different books. See especially *Trade and Credit* (London, 1928), *The Art of Central Banking* (London, 1933), and *Capital and Employment*.
18. Hawtrey, *Trade and Credit*, p. 98.
19. For a careful review of the present state of thinking on this point see R. S. Sayers, "The Rate of Interest as a Weapon of Economic Policy," in *Oxford Studies in the Price Mechanism*, T. Wilson and P. W. S. Andrews, eds. (Oxford, 1951).
20. For a comparison of the two see L. A. Metzler, "Business Cycles and the Modern Theory of Employment," *American Economic Review*, June, 1946, pp. 278-91.
21. Hawtrey, *Trade and Credit*, p. 86.
22. W. H. Beveridge, *Unemployment: A Problem of Industry* (London, 1910), chap. IV.
23. C. O. Hardy, *Risk and Risk-Bearing* (Chicago, 1923), chap. V.
24. A. C. Pigou, *Industrial Fluctuations* (London, 1927), p. 26.
25. See L. K. Frank, "A Theory of Business Cycles," *Quarterly Journal of Economics*, Aug., 1923; T. W. Mitchell, "Competitive Illusion as a Cause of Business Cycles," *Quarterly Journal of Economics*, Aug., 1924; J. A. Hobson, *The Industrial System* (London, 1909); and A. Aftalion, "The Theory of Economic Cycles Based on the Capitalistic Technique of Production," *Review of Economic Statistics*, Oct., 1927.
26. See F. A. Hayck, *Prices and Production* (2nd rev. ed., London, 1935).
27. Abramovitz, *Inventories and Business Cycles*, chap. XIV.

28. R. Nurkse, "The Cyclical Pattern of Inventory Investment," *Quarterly Journal of Economics*, Aug., 1952, 385-408.

CHAPTER THREE

1. For a detailed discussion of various types of period analysis and their implications see A. W. Marget, *The Theory of Prices* (New York, 1942), II, pp. 366-403.

2. Ruth Mack also adopts such a period in one of her recent works. See C. Shoup, M. Friedman, and R. Mack, *Taxing to Prevent Inflation* (New York, 1943), pp. 154-205.

3. Decisions as to prices which are equally important will be considered in some detail in chap. VI.

4. Hansen has recently advanced this as a further condition for equilibrium. Even though planned investment and planned savings are equal, equilibrium will not be reached, he argues, if business firms misjudge the final sales level. Thus if they expect sales to be higher than they actually turn out to be, part of their output will remain unsold and actual investment including this unintended accumulation of inventories will exceed planned investment. But if planned savings and planned investment are interpreted in the schedule sense such a divergence between actual and expected sales would not be possible. Hansen's further condition is already implied in the original equilibrium condition though it is useful to have it spelled out. Hansen reaches this conclusion only because he is thinking of "desired savings" and "desired investment" as plans made in advance rather than schedules relating saving and investment to the level of income. See "The Robertsonian and Swedish Systems of Period Analysis," *Review of Economics and Statistics*, Feb., 1950, p. 28.

5. Hansen defines desired consumption as "that (steady) rate of consumption which would be compatible with the actual level of income *maintained indefinitely over time at a steady rate*" (italics in original).

6. See for example G. Haberler, *Prosperity and Depression* (3rd. ed., Geneva, 1941), p. 457.

7. This sequence is similar to the model developed by Erik Lundberg in *Studies in the Theory of Economic Expansion* (London, 1937), chap. IX. It was later elaborated by L. A. Metzler in "The Nature and Stability of Inventory Cycles," *Review of Economic Statistics*, Aug., 1941.

8. By stable equilibrium is meant a level of income which will continue from one period to the next for some time. It is true, of course, that in the longer view equilibrium will only be stable provided there are no shifts in the consumption function and the level of investment in durable assets continues unchanged. It is also true that over a longer period of time net investment is primarily dependent on growth and change but these features of the economy will be neglected in the present model.

9. See R. Nurkse, "The Cyclical Pattern of Inventory Investment," *Quarterly Journal of Economics*, Aug., 1952, pp. 385-408.

10. There is good reason to believe that Lord Keynes considered this to be the normal case. For, after discussing the possibility of unforeseen increases in investment, he makes the following statement: "Moreover, except in conditions where the consumption industries are already working almost at capacity so that an expansion of output requires an expansion of plant and not merely the more intensive employment of existing plant, there is no reason to suppose that more than a brief interval of time need elapse before employment in the consumption industries is advancing *pari passu* with employment in the capital-goods industries with the multiplier operating near its normal figure." See *The General Theory of Employment Interest and Money* (New York, 1936), p. 124.

11. Some writers have used the concept of income velocity to estimate how soon an increase in consumers' expenditures will result in increased income. But this surely attributes to the business man an undue amount of ignorance. If production plans are related to business men's expectations, it is quite possible to foresee production responding very rapidly to an increase in sales at the retail level. Professor J. W. Angell uses a type of expectations analysis to explain business capital expenditures but fails to extend it to their production plans generally. See *Investment and Business Cycles* (New York, 1946), p. 24.

12. See M. de Chazeau *et al.*, *Jobs and Markets*, Committee for Economic Development Research Study (New York, 1946), p. 24.

13. Metzler, "The Nature and Stability of Inventory Cycles," *Review of Economic Statistics*, pp. 113-29.

14. This point has been discussed in some detail by Abramovitz. See *Inventories and Business Cycles* (New York, 1950), pp. 330-1.

CHAPTER FOUR

1. See J. S. Duesenberry, *Income, Saving and the Theory of Consumer Behavior* (Cambridge, 1949).

2. Simon Kuznets has estimated that in the period 1919 to 1938 in the United States about 77 per cent of all dividends paid to individuals were received by the top 5 per cent of income recipients. See *Shares of Upper Income Groups in Income and Savings* (New York, 1950).

3. Bank of Canada, *Statistical Summary*, Sept., 1951.

4. Federal Reserve System, Board of Governors, *Federal Reserve Bulletin*, Dec. 1945.

5. See L. A. Metzler, "Factors Governing the Length of Inventory Cycles," *Review of Economic Statistics*, Feb., 1947.

6. One widely used type of statistical comparison for published data is the percentage change from the same month of the preceding year. But this affords little indication of changes occurring within a few months. It is easy to show that sales in the current year may continue to exceed the same month of the preceding year for several months after a downturn has started.

7. The individual firm bears a relation to the expansion of all firms which is analogous to the position of a single bank to the whole banking system during an expansion or contraction in deposits.

8. L. A. Metzler, "The Nature and Stability of Inventory Cycles," *Review of Economic Statistics*, Aug., 1941, pp. 113-29.

9. This consideration is similar to that elaborated by J. R. Hicks in *A Contribution to the Theory of the Trade Cycle* (Oxford, 1950), chap. VIII.

10. See M. Abramovitz. *Inventories and Business Cycles* (New York, 1950), pp. 132-53, and the evidence here presented in chap. XI.

11. T. M. Whitin, *The Theory of Inventory Management* (Princeton, 1953), pp. 117-24.

CHAPTER FIVE

1. See L. A. Paradiso, "Classification of Consumer Expenditure by Income Elasticity," *Survey of Current Business*, Jan., 1945.

2. League of Nations, *World Production and Prices, 1936/37* (Geneva, 1937), Appendix I, Table 2, p. 101, and Appendix III, Table I, p. 116.

3. *Ibid.*, Appendix II, Table 1, p. 112.

4. This may also explain why the price of hides shows such a large lead and extreme amplitude in its cyclical fluctuations.

5. League of Nations, *World Production and Prices, 1936/37*, p. 112.

6. However, a survey of Canadian manufacturers made in 1948 showed an almost complete absence of hedging except in the case of grains. The absence of Canadian markets for other commodities coupled with the foreign exchange risk of operating in American markets may explain this.

7. It has been argued that until such an accumulation occurs no sustained recovery can develop because of the bottlenecks that will develop. Since a smaller volume of stocks was sufficient to support a high level of employment it is difficult to see the justification for this point of view. See L. M. Lachmann and F. Snapper, "Commodity Stocks in the Trade Cycle," *Economica*, V (Nov., 1938).

8. See J. M. Keynes, *Treatise on Money* (New York, 1930), I, pp. 282-7, and II, chap. XXVIII. Mr. Hicks has recently accepted Keynes' position that increased output can occur only when a production period has elapsed, but he gives no arguments in support of this assumption. See *A Contribution to the Theory of the Trade Cycle* (Oxford, 1950), pp. 47-51.

9. See R. G. Hawtrey, *The Art of Central Banking* (London, 1933), pp. 389-91.

10. Mr. L. K. Frank was one of the first writers to emphasize this factor and to suggest it as an explanation for the fact that prices fluctuate more violently the further removed they are from the final product. See "A Theory of Business Cycles," *Quarterly Journal of Economics*, Aug., 1923.

CHAPTER SIX

1. See in particular the studies by F. C. Mills, *The Behavior of Prices* (New York, 1927), and *Prices in Recession and Recovery* (New York, 1936).

2. An appraisal of the price policies followed by firms possessing some degree of monopoly is given in *Report of the Royal Commission on Prices* (Ottawa, 1949), II, chap. II. See also U.S. National Resources Committee, *The Structure of the American Economy* (Washington, 1939), I, chap. VIII.

3. See D. Creamer, *Behavior of Wage Rates during Business Cycles* (New York, 1950).

4. See the charts of prices, stocks, and production for a number of primary commodities presented in *Economic Stability in the Post-War World*, Report of the Delegation on Economic Depressions (Geneva, 1945), II, p. 85.

5. This relationship has been discussed at some length by Mr. J. M. Keynes. See *A*

Treatise on Money (New York, 1930), II, chap. XXIX. See also J. B. Williams, "Speculation and the Carryover," *Quarterly Journal of Economics,* May, 1936.

6. Keynes, *Treatise on Money,* II, p. 140.

7. *Ibid.,* p. 136.

8. Keynes' argument neglects the fact that the risk of loss on price declines is at least partially offset by the prospect of gain from a rise in prices. Moreover, there is some evidence that speculators may assume the risk of price change for a negative return. An estimate of the loss or gain from holding wheat from September to May in Canada for the two periods 1904-14 and 1920-30 showed an average net loss, after payment of carrying charges, of 12.9 cents per bushel. Speculators would have made net gains in five years and net losses in fifteen. See Canada, *Report of the Commission to Enquire into Trading in Grain Futures* (Ottawa, 1931), p. 83.

9. Industries which have followed this course of action during the post-war inflationary period are steel, cement, and automobiles. For a discussion of monopoly price policy during this period see F. Machlup, "Misconceptions about the Current Inflation," *Review of Economics and Statistics,* Feb., 1948.

10. Canada, *Report of the Royal Commission on Prices,* III, pp. 107-23. The policy of retail and wholesale stores in respect to markups was discussed in some detail by the Commission. See *ibid.,* II, pp. 229-50, and the discussion of a number of individual industries, *ibid.,* III.

11. This description of his theory is taken from the statement given by Erik Lundberg, *Studies in the Theory of Economic Expansion* (London, 1937), pp. 68-77.

12. See W. C. Mitchell, "Business Cycles," *Readings in Business Cycle Theory* (Philadelphia, 1944), pp. 43-60.

13. The evidence on this point has been carefully examined by Jacob Oser. See "Agricultural Policy and the Business Cycle," *Social Research,* March, 1951.

14. Canada, Dominion Bureau of Statistics, *Inventory Accounting Methods of Canadian Manufacturers* (Ottawa, 1949).

15. A numerical example of the effects of several different accounting methods upon a firm's profits was presented to the Royal Commission on Prices by their accounting adviser; see *Minutes of Proceedings and Evidence* (Ottawa, 1949), pp. 1730-4.

16. The writer's opinion on this point was confirmed by one of the partners in a leading Canadian firm of accountants.

17. This point has been discussed in some detail by K. Lacey in "Profit Measurement and the Trade Cycle," *Economic Journal,* Dec., 1947. Mr. Lacey, suggests a stock replacement reserve as a method of adjusting reported profits to a replacement cost basis.

18. For a discussion of this point see J. K. Butters and P. Niland, *Effects of Taxation: Inventory Accounting and Policies* (Cambridge, 1949), chap. V. It may be noted that the existence of inventory profits and losses increases the built-in flexibility of the government budget.

19. See especially T. Barna, "Valuation of Stocks and the National Income," *Economica,* Nov., 1942, pp. 349-58 and S. Kuznets, "Changing Inventory Valuations and Their Effect on Business Savings and on National Income Produced," *Studies in Income and Wealth* (New York, 1937), I, part IV.

20. Unpublished data from the survey on *Inventory Accounting Methods of Canadian Manufacturers.*

21. Evidence that shoe retailers followed such a practice during 1947 and 1948 was presented in the *Report of the Royal Commission on Prices,* III, p. 219.

CHAPTER SEVEN

1. Canada, Dominion Bureau of Statistics, *Eighth Census of Canada* (Ottawa, 1944), XI, p. 433.

CHAPTER EIGHT

1. This assumes that new natural resources are discovered as rapidly as old ones are depleted or alternatively that those already known will last indefinitely.

2. Mr. G. Haberler, who discusses this point in some detail, concludes that there will usually be some increase in investment. See *Prosperity and Depression* (Geneva, 1941), pp. 99-100.

3. Mr. J. R. Hicks has introduced a limiting concept in his recent model of the trade cycle. See *A Contribution to the Theory of the Trade Cycle* (Oxford, 1950).

4. Professor F. H. Knight has criticized the concept of demand used in the acceleration principle in that it fails to make it a function of price. See "Business Cycle, Interest and Money: A Methodological Approach," *Review of Economic Statistics,* May, 1941, p. 5).

5. This view is shared by A. F. Burns. See "Current Research in Business Cycles: Discussion," *American Economic Review,* May, 1949, p. 80.

6. R. Frisch has pointed out the possibility that under certain circumstances an increase in replacement demand could offset the decline in net investment but this seems an unlikely outcome. See "The Interrelation Between Capital Production and Consumer-Taking," *Journal of Political Economy*, Oct., 1931, and the subsequent discussion in the issues of Dec., 1931, April and Oct., 1932.

7. A number of these considerations have been cited by Mr. M. Kalecki as factors affecting the risk of new investment. See "The Principle of Increasing Risk," *Essays in the Theory of Economic Fluctuations* (London, 1939), pp. 95-106.

8. J. M. Keynes, *The General Theory of Employment Interest and Money* (New York, 1936), p. 109.

9. This argument has recently been supported by S. C. Tsiang in "Accelerator, Theory of the Firm and the Business Cycle," *Quarterly Journal of Economics*, Aug., 1951.

10. R. S. Sayers, "The Springs of Technical Progress in Britain, 1919-1939," *Economic Journal*, June, 1950.

11. See H. B. Arthur, "Inventory Profits in the Business Cycle," *American Economic Review*, March, 1938.

12. It would be a mistake to place too much emphasis on this distinction. Even the investment function II, because of the very nature of dynamic investment, must be of a rather shifting and unstable character. It may shift with the degree of business optimism, the apparent availability of profitable investment outlets, the rate of population growth and many other factors.

13. In his recent discussion of the trade cycle Mr. Hicks uses a model involving real magnitudes but he makes the assumption that the ratio of the price level of investment goods to that of consumption goods is constant. See *A Contribution to the Theory of the Trade Cycle*, p. 11.

14. These conclusions are similar to those reached by Franco Modigliani. See "Fluctuations in the Saving-Income Ratio: A Problem in Economic Forecasting," *Studies in Income and Wealth* (New York, 1949), II, pp. 371-441.

15. The analysis in this study has been mainly in terms of aggregates. No detailed study has been made of the relation of the individual firm to these aggregates. Nevertheless, it may be useful to note here that the equilibrium level of income defined above would be an equilibrium in a more complete sense if the production of each individual firm corresponded to the sales it would receive at this level of income. Otherwise some firms might find themselves faced with undesired additions to their stocks that would be offset by unplanned reductions in stocks for other firms.

16. No attempt is made to combine the savings and investment functions advanced here into a model of the business cycle similar to that advanced by Mr. N. Kaldor, for it is doubtful if the functions intersect in the particular way obtained by Kaldor. However, the reader may wish to try experimenting with such a model. See "A Model of the Trade Cycle," *Economic Journal*, March, 1940.

17. M. Abramovitz, *Inventories and Business Cycles* (New York, 1950), chap. V.

CHAPTER TEN

1. See A. F. Burns and W. C. Mitchell, *Measuring Business Cycles* (New York, 1946), pp. 71-114.

2. For a description of these attempts at price stabilization see J. A. Guthrie, *The Newsprint Paper Industry* (Cambridge, 1941), chap. VIII, and V. W. Bladen, *An Introduction to Political Economy* (Toronto, 1941), chap. VI.

3. The use of actual cost in determining selling prices may be related to the industry's practice of selling under annual contracts.

4. Data from Bank of Canada, *Statistical Summary: 1946 Supplement*. Methods used in preparing the estimate of inventory revaluation were similar to those used by T. Barna. See "Valuation of Stocks and the National Income," *Economica*, Nov., 1942.

5. Canada, Report of Combines Commissioner, *Canada and International Cartels* (Ottawa, 1945), pp. 25-35.

6. See *Report of the Royal Commission on Price Spreads* (Ottawa, 1935), pp. 50-4.

7. See Department of Labour, *Investigation into an Alleged Combine of Tobacco Manufacturers and Other Buyers of Raw Leaf Tobacco in the Province of Ontario* (Ottawa, 1933) and W. E. Haviland, "Major Developments in the Marketing of Leaf Tobacco in Ontario," *Economic Annalist*, Feb., 1951.

8. See Haviland, *ibid.*, p. 7.

9. One year's crop is not fully reflected in the manufacturer's reported inventory until the following year. Purchases are made in the fall of the year but delivery may not occur until the next year.

10. Canada, House of Commons, Special Committee on Price Spreads and Mass Buying, *Minutes of Proceedings and Evidence* (Ottawa, 1934), II, p. 1590.

11. Canada, House of Commons, Special Committee on Farm Implement Prices, *Minutes of Proceedings and Evidence* (Ottawa, 1937), p. 20, p. 44, p. 560, and p. 623.

12. *Ibid.*, pp. 346-8.

13. A more detailed description of this industry is given in the *Report of the Royal Commission on Prices* (Ottawa, 1949), III, chap. V.

14. Royal Commission on Price Spreads, *Minutes of Proceedings and Evidence*, p. 3416.

15. *Ibid.*, p. 3148.

16. *Ibid.*, p. 3263.

17. See the references given in chap. II above.

CHAPTER ELEVEN

1. Canada, Dominion Bureau of Statistics, *National Accounts: Income and Expenditure, 1926-1950* (Ottawa, 1952), pp. 56-7.

2. See Statistical Appendix, Table XII.

3. M. Abramovitz, *Inventories and Business Cycles* (New York, 1950), pp. 1-8.

4. *Ibid.*, pp. 481-2.

5. *Ibid.*, pp. 110-6.

6. Data on department stores' sales and inventories were obtained from Canada, House of Commons, Special Committee on Price Spreads and Mass Buying, *Minutes of Proceedings and Evidence*, II and III. Data on chain stores were taken from Canada, Dominion Bureau of Statistics, *Retail Chain Stores, 1949* (Ottawa, 1950).

7. Keynes has argued that the change in physical quantity is the more significant but the author can see no basis for this conclusion. Cf. Keynes' statement "The addition to the carry-over is an addition to current investment. This conclusion is not invalidated if prices fall sharply." (*The General Theory of Employment Interest and Money* (New York, 1936) p. 330.)

8. See *Report of the Royal Grain Inquiry Commission* (Ottawa, 1938), pp. 33-8.

9. For an account of these price stabilization measures see the *Report of the Royal Grain Inquiry Commission*, chap. VII.

10. Farm inventories also include livestock held on the farm. Explanation of their fluctuations would require analysis of the hog and beef cycles.

INDEX

Lightning Source UK Ltd.
Milton Keynes UK
UKHW030613210722
406167UK00006B/672

9 781442 651647